SSAT Middle Level
Practice Tests

SSAT Middle Level Practice Tests

Three Full-Length Verbal and Quantitative
Mock Tests with Detailed Answer Explanations

ANTHEM PRESS

Anthem Press
An imprint of Wimbledon Publishing Company
www.anthempress.com

This edition first published in UK and USA 2024
by ANTHEM PRESS
75–76 Blackfriars Road, London SE1 8HA, UK
or PO Box 9779, London SW19 7ZG, UK
and
244 Madison Ave #116, New York, NY 10016, USA

© 2024

British Library Cataloguing-in-Publication Data
A catalogue record for this book is available from the British Library.

Library of Congress Control Number: 2023949174
A catalog record for this book has been requested.

ISBN-13: 978-1-83999-094-6 (Pbk)
ISBN-10: 1-83999-094-5 (Pbk)

This title is also available as an e-book.

Contents

Introduction

About SSAT

The Secondary School Admission Test (SSAT) is a standardized test used by admission officers to assess the abilities of students seeking to enroll in an independent school. The SSAT measures the basic verbal, math, and reading skills students need for successful performance in independent schools. Every year, 80,000+ students take the SSAT to apply to independent schools. There are two types of SSAT administrations.

Grade Level

Students of grades 3–11 can register for one of the three SSAT tests, depending on their grades:

- The Elementary Level test is for students currently in grades 3 and 4.
- The Middle Level test is for students currently in grades 5–7.
- The Upper Level test is for students currently in grades 8–11.

The SSAT Middle has five sections (in order of testing): The structure of the test has two separate Math sections.

The SSAT Middle level paper structure is as below:

Section 1: Writing Sample—1 qs / 25 mins
10 mins break
Section 2: Quantitative Math—25 qs / 30 mins
Section 3: Reading Comprehension—40 qs / 40 mins
10 mins break
Section 4: Verbal Reasoning—60 qs / 30 mins
Section 5: Quantitative Math—25 qs / 30 mins

How does a student arrange to take the SSAT?

Students may take the SSAT in one of the following ways:

1. **Paper SSAT:** This is the most popular and preferred option. Parents can register for the paper-based test by creating an account on https://portal.ssat.org/SAP/Tests/NewRegistration.

2. **Flex Testing:** This increases the availability of the paper SSAT beyond the standard testing dates. Consider Flex testing when the standard dates or locations don't work for your schedule. There are two types of Flex testing:

   - Open Flex tests—are when a school hosts a group of students for Flex testing and makes registration open to the public.

   - Closed Flex tests—are when an educational consultant or school administers the SSAT to an individual or a small group of students.

3. **At-Home Testing:** The SSAT at Home is a computer-based version of the SSAT taken on designated testing dates at pre-scheduled times.

4. **The Prometric SSAT:** This is a secure, computer-based version of the SSAT taken at Prometric test centers. It is the same reliable test as the paper and SSAT at Home versions. Note that SSAT Elementary Level is not offered by Prometric.

What types of questions are on the SSAT?

The first section, Writing Sample, requires the student to respond to a preselected writing prompt and the next four sections are composed of multiple-choice questions.

The Quantitative Math and Verbal Reasoning section measures the applicant's reasoning ability.

In the next section, Reading Comprehension, the student is asked to read a passage and then answer items specific to that passage.

The Verbal Reasoning test consists of two types of items: vocabulary and sentence completion.

At the Middle Level, the Quantitative Math test conforms to national mathematics standards and asks the student to identify the problem and find a solution to it. The items require one or more steps in calculating the answer.

The table below gives a quick snapshot of the questions in the SSAT:

Test Section	Questions	Time	Details
Writing Sample	1 Question	25 minutes	The writing sample is not scored, but schools use it to assess writing skills.
Quantitative Math	25 Questions	30 minutes	Multiple-choice questions composed of math computation based on grade-level math topics.
Reading Comprehension	40 Questions	40 minutes	Reading passages with multiple-choice questions based on the reading passages.
Verbal Comprehension	60 Questions	30 minutes	Vocabulary and analogy questions.
Quantitative Math	25 Questions	30 minutes	Multiple-choice questions composed of math computation based on grade-level math topics.

What is the format of the test? All questions are multiple choice

What is the medium of the test? Computer based

How to use the book?

- Before you start the test, read the directions for each section and note the time allocated.
- Ensure that you have a continuous block of time available to complete the entire test—including all the sections.
- When you take the practice test, remove all possible distractions, including your phone.
- Take the entire test in one sitting—this is very critical for getting a realistic view of how you would do in the real test.

- Check your answers right after the test.
- Review the explanations on the same day, so you remember why you chose a particular answer.
- Before starting the next practice test, review the answers that you got wrong from the previous test and the explanations, so you don't make the same mistakes.

SSAT Results

Use these attached sample reports to familiarize yourself with the SSAT score reports. You'll also find detailed explanations of each section below. There are two types of scores:

SSAT Scaled Scores: Each of the three main Elementary Level test sections is scored on a scale of 300 to 600, with a total scaled score range of 900 to 1800. Each of the three main Middle Level test sections is scored on a scale of 440 to 710, with a total scaled score range of 1,320 to 2,130. Each of the three main Upper Level test sections is scored on a scale of 500 to 800, with a total scaled score range of 1,500 to 2,400.

SSAT Percentiles: SSAT percentile rankings range between 1% and 99% and show how a student performed as compared to the other students in the same grade and of the same gender who have taken the SSAT during the past three years.

Learn more about SSAT scoring here: https://www.ssat.org/about/scoring/ssat-score-report

SSAT Middle Level Exam 1

WRITING SAMPLE

Time—25 minutes

Directions:

Read the following topics carefully. Take a few minutes to select the topic you find more interesting. Think about the topic and organize your thoughts on a scrap paper before you begin writing.

Topic A: When I grow up, I want to be …

Topic B: If I were to move to another place, I …

Circle your selection: Topic A or Topic B. Write your essay on the selected topic on the paper provided. Your essay should NOT exceed two pages and must be written in pencil. Be sure that your handwriting is legible and that you must stay within the lines and margins.

SECTION 2

QUANTITATIVE MATH

Time—30 minutes
25 Questions

In this section, there are five possible answers after each problem. Choose which one is best.

Example

5,413 – 4,827 =

(A) 586
(B) 596
(C) 696
(D) 1,586
(E) 1,686

Answer

● Ⓑ Ⓒ Ⓓ Ⓔ

The correct answer to this question is lettered A, so space A is marked.

---

1. Find the median of the dataset. Round off to the nearest tenth, if applicable. {78, 72, 80, 83, 79, 81}

(A) 79.5   (B) 79   (C) 80   (D) 81   (E) 78

2. Find the range of this set of numbers: 245, 698, 503, 849, 415

(A) 434   (B) 415   (C) 245   (D) 283   (E) 604

3. Please refer to the chart below:

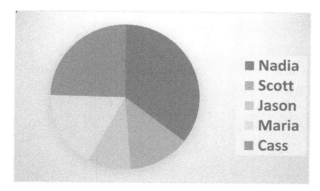

Five mayoral candidates ran for Kling City. The chart shows the share of votes that each candidate won. Which of the following would be the most reasonable estimate of the percent of the vote for Nadia?

(A) 35%   (B) 20%   (C) 5%   (D) 10%   (E) 15%

4. In which quadrant or on which axis of the coordinate plane will you find the point (3, –5)?

    (A) quadrant I   (B) quadrant II   (C) quadrant III   (D) quadrant IV   (E) none of the above

5. Find the area of the trapezoid.

    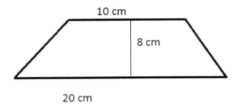

    (A) 105 cm²   (B) 110 cm²   (C) 90 cm²   (D) 120 cm²   (E) 100 cm²

6. Which of the following expressions is equivalent to the expression $-7(-2g + 9)$?

    (A) $-14g + 63$ (B) $-14g - 63$ (C) $14g - 63$ (D) $14g + 63$ (E) $14g - 9$

7. Express the quotient as a fraction in lowest terms: $4\frac{1}{5} \div 5\frac{3}{5}$

    (A) $\frac{105}{140}$ (B) $\frac{3}{4}$ (C) $\frac{140}{105}$ (D) $\frac{4}{3}$ (E) $\frac{3}{7}$

8. If $C = 12$, then what is $4C + 4$?

    (A) 40   (B) 48   (C) 52   (D) 44   (E) 42

9. Evaluate: $\frac{3}{5} \times \frac{2}{6}$

    (A) $\frac{1}{3}$ (B) $\frac{1}{5}$ (C) $\frac{1}{6}$ (D) $\frac{2}{10}$ (E) $\frac{2}{6}$

10. A clothing store sells a certain coat for $40. During the holidays, it offers a sale where the new price of the coat is now $30. What percent discount is the store selling the coat for?

    (A) 40%   (B) 20%   (C) 10%   (D) 25%   (E) 35%

11. Maureen will be visiting an orphanage today. She wants to give 2 slices of pizza to each of the 14 children. How many pizzas should she buy if each pizza has 8 slices?

    (A) 4 pizzas   (B) 3 pizzas   (C) 5 pizzas   (D) 1 pizza   (E) 2 pizzas

12. What's 20% of 420?

    (A) 126   (B) 105   (C) 84   (D) 63   (E) 80

13. Four candidates ran for mayor of Rayon City. The results are below:

Van Claude	2,631
Montemayor	1,747
Delos Reyes	8,903
Clemente	3,579

According to the city ordinance, a candidate must win more than 50% of the total number of votes to win the election; if this does not happen, the two candidates who win the most votes will face each other in a runoff election. Based on the table above, which of the following is the outcome of the vote?

(A) Clemente and Van Claude will face each other in a runoff

(B) Montemayor won the election outright

(C) Van Claude and Delos Reyes will face each other in a runoff

(D) Clemente won the election outright   (E) Delos Reyes won the election outright

14. Solve for x: $5x - 42 = 53$

(A) 15   (B) 19   (C) 20   (D) 18   (E) 21

15. Simplify: $(3x + 6) - (8x - 4)$

(A) $-5x + 10$ (B) $5x + 10$ (C) $-5x - 10$ (D) $5x - 10$ (E) $-5x + 5$

For questions 16 and 17, refer to the given set below:

{74, 67, 80, 72, 76, 73, 90, 68}

16. What is the mean of the set?

(A) 73   (B) 75   (C) 77   (D) 74   (E) 76

17. What is the median of the set?

(A) 15   (B) 19   (C) 20   (D) 18   (E) 21

18. Find the range of this set: 478, 640, 319, 802, 732

(A) 483   (B) 324   (C) 478   (D) 319   (E) 438

19. What is the mode for the following set of numbers? 1, 2, 2, 5, 8, 8, 11, 12, 12, 12, 25, 28

(A) 12   (B) 11   (C) 8   (D) 2   (E) 28

20. A right triangle has one leg with a length of 6 ft and a hypotenuse of 10 ft. What is the length of the other leg?

(A) 9 ft   (B) 2 ft   (C) 8 ft   (D) 4 ft   (E) 10 ft

21. See the Venn diagram below. Which of the following sets is represented by the gray region?

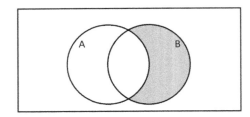

   (A) $\overline{A} \cup \overline{B}$ (B) $\overline{A} \cap B$ (C) $A \cap \overline{B}$ (D) $\overline{A} \cup B$ (E) $\overline{A} \cap \overline{B}$

22. Which of the following is a subset of the set A = {x | x is a multiple of 4}?
   (A) 12, 16, 20   (B) 12, 15, 20   (C) 8, 12, 14   (D) 20, 22, 24   (E) 20, 24, 30

23. A square has perimeter 144 in. What is the length of one side?
   (A) 4 in   (B) 36 in   (C) 30 in   (D) 35 in   (E) 144 in

24. A triangle has base 20 in and height 15 in. What is its area?
   (A) 300 in²   (B) 100 in²   (C) 200 in²   (D) 150 in²   (E) 120 in²

25. Which of the following is an example of an application of the distributive property?
   (A) 10 × (29 × 17) = (10 × 29) × 17
   (B) 10 + (29 × 17) = 10 + (17 × 29)
   (C) 10 × (29 + 17) = 10 × 29 + 10 × 17
   (D) 10 + (29 × 17) = (29 × 17) + 10
   (E) none of the above

SECTION 3

READING COMPREHENSION

Time—40 minutes
40 Questions

Read each passage carefully and then answer the questions about it. For each question, decide on the basis of the passage which one of the choices best answers the question.

Who looks at a banana peel and thinks, "I could turn that into plastic"? Elif Bilgin, for one. At age 16, the high school student from Istanbul, Turkey, even won a 2013 Google Science Fair award for her plan to turn banana peels into a bioplastic.

The word "bioplastic" can be used to describe a plastic that is biodegradable, meaning it breaks down over time. But the word also refers to a plastic made with renewable resources such as vegetable oils, starches, and other biology-based ingredients. Some, but not all, plastics made of renewable resources are also biodegradable.

In her project description, Elif explains that she wanted to work with bioplastics because they could help to reduce air, land, and water pollution caused by traditional plastics, which are made with petroleum.

It took her 10 tries over the course of two years, but she finally came up with a way to make a banana-peel plastic that is sturdy and stable enough to be used in such products as artificial limbs and cable insulation. She reports that her method was simple enough that people "could actually do it at home," meaning that, at least in theory, "anyone could use this plastic."

Elif says she loves doing scientific research, and one of her inspirations is Marie Curie, the Nobel Prize-winning physicist who studied radioactivity. She hopes to do more projects that could be good for the environment. Her biggest dream? To one day build a "greenhouse made of waste materials."

She also hopes to study medicine one day, a goal she says the money from her science fair award can help her reach. More important, she says, is that winning proves she's on the right path, and "science is my calling."

From Istanbul Teen Creates Bioplastic from Bananas *by Kids Discover*

1. Who is Elif Bilgin?

    (A) the Nobel Prize-winning physicist who studied radioactivity

    (B) a college student who discovered bioplastics

    (C) a high school student who turned potato peels into bioplastics

    (D) a high school student who turned banana peels into bioplastics

2. Which of the following is the meaning of the word "bioplastic"?

(A) a biodegradable plastic

(B) a non-biodegradable plastic

(C) a living plastic

(D) plastic made of reused plastics

3. What object was turned into plastic in the article?

(A) potato skin   (B) banana peel   (C) vegetable oil   (D) flaxseeds

4. Why did the high school student started working with bioplastics?

(A) because they cannot afford plastic bags

(B) because she's planning to start a business

(C) because they could help to reduce air, land, and water pollution caused by traditional plastics

(D) because nobody does

5. How long did it take for Elif to successfully make a bioplastic?

(A) one week

(B) one semester off school

(C) the process took her 10 tries over the course of two years

(D) two months

6. Who was Elif's inspiration that made her love doing scientific research?

(A) Marie Curie   (B) Marie Curi   (C) Mari Curie   (D) Marie Cure

Your brain forms, organizes, and stores memories in the hippocampus. This tiny organ helps you form long-term memories, connect memories to other memories, and connect memories to emotions and senses. When you smell cookies and think of your grandma—or maybe the mall—that's the hippocampus at work.

The name comes from the Greek words for seahorse, because the organ is shaped kind of like one (hippo means horse and kampos means sea). The organ consists of two parts: one on the right side of your brain and one on the left. It sits near the amygdala and the pineal gland, inside the temporal lobe.

The hippocampus helps you navigate, orient yourself in space, and form emotional reactions. In people who suffer from Alzheimer's Disease, it's among the first parts of the brain to become damaged, which explains why these folks have a hard time remembering things and may get lost easily.

It can also be damaged by oxygen deprivation, infection, inflammation caused by epilepsy, and stress. Someone with a damaged hippocampus may be able to remember new things but not recall older memories. In some cases, a damaged hippocampus can even block formation of new memories. Because the hippocampus is very sensitive to stress, experiencing high degrees of stress for a long time can lead to shrinking of this important organ.

Yet studies show that a damaged hippocampus does not prevent a person from learning new skills, so that function is most likely controlled by other areas of the brain. The fact is that the brain is still very <u>mysterious</u>, so while we may know a lot about it, we don't yet even know how much we don't know.

From Meet the Hippocampus, Where Memories Go to Make Sense *by Kids Discover*

7. What is the hippocampus?

   (A) a tiny organ that helps you form long-term memories, connect memories to other memories, and connect memories to emotions and senses

   (B) sponge-like, cone-shaped structures that fill most of the chest cavity

   (C) lies on the right side of the abdominal cavity beneath the diaphragm

   (D) a muscular organ located in the pelvic cavity

8. What is the origin of the name hippocampus?

   (A) from the Greek word for cuckoo—"kokkux"—because the curved shape of the bone resembles the bird's beak

   (B) comes from the Greek words for seahorse because the organ is shaped kind of like one

   (C) from the Latin and Greek word "arteria," which means "air holder"

   (D) from the Latin word "palma" from the palm tree

9. Where is the hippocampus located?

   (A) at the back of your throat

   (B) lying crosswise in the abdominal cavity beneath the diaphragm

   (C) near the amygdala and the pineal gland, inside the temporal lobe

   (D) at the front of your thigh that crosses both the hip and knee joints

10. What can damage the hippocampus?

   (A) prolonged exposure to sunlight

   (B) delayed puberty

   (C) not eating on time

   (D) oxygen deprivation, infection, inflammation

11. What is the meaning of the underlined word "mysterious"?

   (A) uncomplicated and easy to do or understand

   (B) truthful and straightforward; frank

   (C) not having any extra detail or explanation; plain or blunt

   (D) difficult or impossible to understand, explain, or identify

12. When someone's hippocampus is damaged, we can infer that he/she?

    (A) may make sudden movements

    (B) may forget the way home

    (C) may lose the ability to control their breathing

    (D) may uncontrollably blink his/her eyes

13. Which among the choices below is not one of the functions of the hippocampus?

    (A) form long-term memories

    (B) connect memories to other memories

    (C) produce the happy hormone

    (D) connect memories to emotions and senses

me and you be sisters.
we be the same.

me and you
coming from the same place.

me and you
be greasing our legs
touching up our edges.

me and you
be scared of rats
be stepping on roaches.

me and you
come running high down <u>purdy</u> street one time
and mama laugh and shake her head at
me and you.
me and you
got babies
got thirty-five
got black
let our hair go back
be loving ourselves
be loving ourselves
be sisters.
only where you sing,
I poet.

From sisters *by Lucille Clifton*

14. What is the author talking about in her poem?

(A) the relationship of two sisters and their life experiences that they shared as they grew older

(B) the bittersweet of love the second time

(C) gift of second chances

(D) finding your soulmates

15. What mood is implied in the poem?

(A) blissful (B) sad (C) morose (D) lethargic

16. What is being implied on stanza 6?

(A) growing apart

(B) got dirty from the cinder

(C) growing old together

(D) became single parents

17. Which is synonymous to the underlined word "purdy"?

(A) undesirable (B) unpleasant (C) ugly (D) pretty

18. What does the line "coming from the same place" most likely mean?

(A) from the same hospital

(B) from the same drop-off point

(C) spent the same childhood

(D) took from the same pages of the book

Your heart is divided up into four chambers: two ventricles and two atria. As your heart beats, doors open and close between the different chambers, so the blood moves one way and not the other. The atria sit at the top of the heart and work as blood collection chambers. There are <u>floppy</u>, wrinkled-looking pouches on either atrium, waiting to expand as blood flows into them. These are the auricles, and they get their name from the Latin word for ear. We think they sort of look like the ears on a puppy.

From The Seahorse In Your Brain: Where Body Parts Got Their Names *by Joy Ho, Erin Ross*

19. What is the article about?

(A) the lungs and its parts

(B) the heart and its parts

(C) the atria and its parts

(D) the location of the heart

20. How many chambers does the heart have?

(A) one (B) three (C) four (D) two

21. Where does the word "auricle" come from?

(A) named after a similar-looking flute

(B) Latin for "really big hole"

(C) named after goats because some people have tufts of hair on the tragus like goats do on their chins

(D) from the Latin word for ear which looks like the ears on a puppy

22. Which one best describes the article?

(A) educational (B) persuasive (C) entertaining (D) argumentative

23. What does the underlined word "floppy" mean?

(A) rigidly upright or straight

(B) tending to hang or move in a limp, loose

(C) swell with blood, water, or another fluid

(D) not easily bent or changed in shape

> The mountain and the squirrel
> Had a quarrel,
> And the former called the <u>latter</u>
> "Little prig."
> Bun replied,
> "You are doubtless very big;
> But all sorts of things and weather
> Must be taken in together
> To make up a year
> And a sphere.
> And I think it no disgrace
> To occupy my place.
> If I'm not so large as you,
> You are not so small as I,
> And not half so spry:
> I'll not deny you make
> A very pretty squirrel track.
> Talents differ; all is well and wisely put;
> If I cannot carry forests on my back,
> <u>Neither</u> can you crack a nut."

From The Mountain and the Squirrel *by Ralph Waldo Emerson*

24. What is the meaning behind the poem?

   (A) how tall mountains are and abundant with nuts

   (B) where squirrels live

   (C) about what squirrels eat

   (D) nature and how living things depend on what the nature gives

25. What is the mood of the poem?

   (A) argumentative (B) cheerful (C) light-hearted (D) calm

26. What does the underlined word "latter" mean?

   (A) happening or doing something at the agreed or proper time

   (B) at a time in the near future; soon or afterward

   (C) the first or first mentioned of two people or things

   (D) the second or second mentioned of two people or things

27. Which is the "latter" in the poem?

   (A) weather (B) mountain (C) squirrel (D) nut

28. What of the words below is a synonym of "crack"?

   (A) snap (B) unite (C) merge (D) combine

29. What part of speech is the word "neither"?

   (A) adverb (B) noun (C) pronoun (D) verb

Hannah Parmenter, who is now 21, got a serious concussion when she was 11 while playing soccer. She still has problems from the concussion today.

1.7 million to 3 million young people get concussions every year from playing sports. Doctors used to think that rest was the best treatment for concussions in children. But these days, researchers think that returning to school soon after a concussion might be better. Children who missed less school had fewer problems after two weeks. This means that returning to school and daily life may help the brain recover.

Doctors recommend that parents with children who get concussions should help them socialize, not miss too much school, sleep well, and do light exercise. The research shows that doctors can help kids with concussions, and they should not just wait for them to get better.

From Young people and concussion *by News in levels*

30. What is the main topic of the article?

(A) about how children get concussions

(B) about the latest discovery that researchers think that returning to school might be better than resting and missing school

(C) about where children should go if they get concussions

(D) about the latest discovery that researchers think that resting and missing school is better

31. Which best describes the article?

(A) solemn   (B) argumentative   (C) informative   (D) cheerful

32. What is the recent advice of doctors when children get concussions as opposed to before?

(A) rest from school   (B) return to school and daily life   (C) house arrest   (D) go on vacation

33. Why do doctors recommend to let children not delay returning to school?

(A) it may decrease the time they need to catch up on lessons

(B) it may help teachers stay on track of lessons

(C) it may help parents continue their daily activities

(D) it may help the brain recover

34. What does the underlined word "recover" mean?

(A) become progressively worse

(B) diminish in strength or quality

(C) return to a normal state of health

(D) rot or decompose through the action of bacteria and fungi

35. What is the synonym of the word "socialize"?

(A) interact   (B) isolate   (C) imprison   (D) arrest

When the scale tells me I've not gained a pound
When my glasses or phone or keys have been found,
When the cop pulls me over but spares me the ticket
When my ice cream cone drips and I get to lick it,
When I read the obituaries and don't know a soul,
When the car just ahead of me pays for my toll,
When my pants can fit without sucking my gut in
When I'm on the dance floor and a man asks to cut in,
When it's time for a movie and I get to choose it,
When I cut out the coupon and remember to use it.
Everyone understands the worth
Of a big celebration: a marriage, a birth
But moments of joy, too many to mention
Brighten each day, when we just pay attention.

From When Is That Golden Moment? *by Eileen Hession*

36. What is the main message of the poem?

   (A) the golden moment is the biggest break of your life

   (B) not every little thing is a reason to celebrate

   (C) the golden moment is a matter of perception, and one must be grateful for the little moments of joy

   (D) little moments of joy come and go

37. What is the author's mood as implied by the poem?

   (A) melancholic   (B) grateful   (C) apologetic   (D) grieving

38. What does the underlined word "spares" mean?

   (A) assign responsibility for a fault or wrong

   (B) refrain from inflicting (something) on (someone)

   (C) hold someone firmly in a specified position so they are unable to move

   (D) form and express a sophisticated judgment of

39. What is the synonym of the word "gain"?

   (A) put on   (B) drop   (C) elude   (D) dodge

40. Which best fits the mood of the poem?

   (A) when you have to go back to class for your lost pen

   (B) when you happen to have spare change for the bus in your jacket

   (C) when you hit your foot on the edge of the bed

   (D) when you fell out of your bed from the loud screaming of your neighbor

SECTION 4

VERBAL REASONING

Time—30 minutes
60 Questions

This section consists of two different types of questions. There are directions for each type.

Each of the following questions consists of one word followed by four words or phrases. You are to select a word or phrase whose meaning is closest to the word in capital letters.

Example

SWIFT: (A) clean   (B) fancy   (C) fast   (D) quiet

Answer

(A) (B) ● (D)

---

1. ADAPT

   (A) adjust   (B) neglect   (C) reject   (D) disarrange

2. ADMIRE

   (A) blame   (B) adore   (C) denounce   (D) hate

3. AIM

   (A) ignore   (B) forget   (C) target   (D) neglect

4. ANALYZE

   (A) forget   (B) ignore   (C) assemble   (D) inspect

5. ASSURE

   (A) discourage   (B) dissuade   (C) distress   (D) encourage

6. BARREN

   (A) damp   (B) moist   (C) empty   (D) productive

7. BEAT

   (A) caress   (B) hit   (C) soft   (D) tickle

8. COMPEL

(A) force   (B) free   (C) allow   (D) decide

9. COMPREHEND

(A) understand   (B) deny   (C) decline   (D) reject

10. DRAFT

(A) final   (B) outline   (C) boat   (D) mad

11. DURATION

(A) distance   (B) period   (C) weight   (D) donation

12. DEBATE

(A) agree   (B) endorse   (C) discuss   (D) accept

13. EAGER

(A) apathetic   (B) disinterested   (C) bored   (D) enthusiastic

14. ENVY

(A) jealousy   (B) sympathy   (C) kindness   (D) generosity

15. EXCAVATE

(A) live   (B) fill   (C) dig   (D) load

16. FORTUNATE

(A) hapless   (B) lucky   (C) pitiful   (D) unlucky

17. FRANK

(A) direct   (B) secretive   (C) liar   (D) discreet

18. GAP

(A) headgear   (B) vent   (C) smooth   (D) closing

19. HOARD

(A) reset   (B) store   (C) eliminate   (D) waste

20. HOMELY

(A) near (B) far (C) comfortable (D) uncomfortable

21. IMPLY

(A) direct (B) exclude (C) mean (D) immediate

22. INHABIT

(A) live (B) leave (C) abandon (D) sell

23. INQUIRY

(A) answer (B) query (C) paper (D) grocery

24. JUDGE

(A) start (B) conclude (C) commence (D) begin

25. JUSTIFY

(A) explain (B) condemn (C) demand (D) conclude

26. KEEP

(A) throw (B) waste (C) eliminate (D) pile

27. LEGEND

(A) research (B) investigation (C) tale (D) marker

28. LIBERATE

(A) confine (B) enslave (C) capture (D) release

29. LURE

(A) deter (B) defer (C) lose (D) tempt

30. MEDDLE

(A) interfere (B) enjoy (C) embrace (D) distance

The following questions ask you to find the relationships between words. For each question, select the choice that best completes the meaning of the sentence.

Example

Ann carried the box carefully so that she would not _____ the pretty glasses.

(A) break   (B) fix   (C) open   (D) stop

Answer
● (B) (C) (D)

---

31. Good is better as bad is to

(A) unkind   (B) evil   (C) badder   (D) worse

32. Knife is to sharp as hammer is to

(A) nail   (B) carpenter   (C) tool   (D) blunt

33. Farthest is to far as last is to

(A) late   (B) final   (C) line   (D) order

34. Little is to child as old is to

(A) years   (B) age   (C) grandparent   (D) young

35. Few is to fewer as many is to

(A) several   (B) more   (C) count   (D) people

36. Big is to bigger as little is to

(A) littler   (B) tiny   (C) kid   (D) size

37. Bacon is protein as bread is to

(A) toasted   (B) wheat   (C) sliced   (D) carbohydrate

38. Apple is to fruit as broccoli is to

(A) cauliflower   (B) green   (C) vegetable   (D) hard

39. Turn on is to turn off as jump in is to

(A) pool   (B) verb   (C) jump out   (D) preposition

40. Above is to below as front is to

   (A) door   (B) entrance   (C) face   (D) back

41. Absent is present as abundant is to

   (A) scarce   (B) plentiful   (C) harvest   (D) fertile

42. Far is to further and late is to

   (A) time   (B) latter   (C) class   (D) expired

43. Banana is to fruit as bean is to

   (A) pods   (B) green   (C) vegetable   (D) long

44. Cold ham is to protein as yoghurt is to

   (A) pasteurized   (B) strawberry   (C) white   (D) dairy

45. Spacious is to wide as close is to

   (A) pride   (B) shut   (C) wild   (D) ferocious

46. Leave is to abandon as hug is to

   (A) push   (B) verb   (C) embrace   (D) tight

47. Rude is to impolite as mad is to

   (A) insane   (B) sane   (C) mind   (D) criminal

48. Accept is to refuse as borrow is to

   (A) ask   (B) lend   (C) pencil   (D) verb

49. Accurate is to inaccurate as capable is to

   (A) incapable   (B) able   (C) knowledgeable   (D) skillful

50. Bold is to timid as brave is to

   (A) strong   (B) coward   (C) adjective   (D) knight

51. Her is female as his to

   (A) him   (B) male   (C) pronoun   (D) person

52. Cereal is to breakfast as steak is to

    (A) dinner (B) meat (C) beef (D) medium rare

53. Sandwich is to lunch as egg is to

    (A) poultry (B) fried (C) breakfast (D) brown

54. Baker is to bakery as post man is to

    (A) male (B) post office (C) letter (D) occupation

55. Cooking oil is to liquid as catsup bottle is to

    (A) solid (B) glass (C) plastic (D) broken

56. Florist is to flower as chef is to

    (A) kitchen (B) food (C) hat (D) restaurant

57. Hair stylist is to hair as lyricist is to

    (A) artist (B) occupation (C) studio (D) lyrics

58. Heat is to summer as snow is to

    (A) winter (B) cold (C) white (D) December

59. Kettle is to hot water as freezer is to

    (A) cold (B) refrigerator (C) ice cubes (D) frozen

60. Beans is to coffee as leaves is to

    (A) tea (B) plant (C) green (D) organic

SECTION 5

QUANTITATIVE MATH

Time—30 minutes

25 Questions

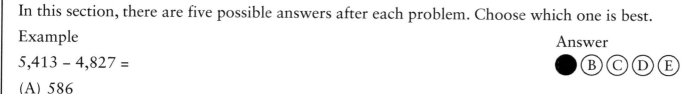

In this section, there are five possible answers after each problem. Choose which one is best.

Example

$5{,}413 - 4{,}827 =$

(A) 586
(B) 596
(C) 693
(D) 1,586
(E) 1,686

The correct answer to this question is lettered A, so space A is marked.

Answer

● (B) (C) (D) (E)

1. Find the perimeter of the square.

7.3 cm

(A) 29.5 cm   (B) 29.2 cm   (C) 22.9 cm   (D) 25.9 cm   (E) 29.3 cm

2. Give the mean of the dataset (round it off to the nearest tenth, if applicable): {77, 73, 56, 98, 78, 85}

(A) 77.8   (B) 77.5   (C) 77.9   (D) 77.6   (E) 77.7

3. What is the median of the following numbers: 3, 3, 3, 9, 12, 15, 15, 18, 21

(A) 9   (B) 3   (C) 15   (D) 12   (E) 21

4. Find the mode in this set: 1648, 5971, 5971, 5846, 5846, 5971, 1648, 3003, 3003, 5971

(A) 1648   (B) 5846   (C) 3003   (D) 5917   (E) 5971

5. Simplify the expression: $5(z + 16)$

(A) $5z + 40$ (B) $5z - 40$ (C) $5z + 80$ (D) $5z - 80$ (E) $z + 80$

6. Evaluate: $4\frac{2}{9} - 2\frac{1}{9} + 3\frac{7}{9}$

   (A) $5\frac{5}{9}$ (B) $5\frac{8}{9}$ (C) $5\frac{1}{9}$ (D) $5\frac{7}{9}$ (E) $5\frac{2}{9}$

7. The sales tax rate for a particular locality is 9%. How much will be paid after adding the tax for $172.43 worth of groceries?

   (A) $187.95 (B) $187.59 (C) $178.95 (D) $178.59 (E) $188.95

8. Evaluate: $\frac{16}{5} \div \frac{4}{25}$

   (A) 50 (B) 100 (C) 200 (D) 10 (E) 20

9. 340 is 25% of what number?

   (A) 1360 (B) 1630 (C) 1020 (D) 680 (E) 1200

10. Lola bought $\frac{1}{8}$ of an acre for $2,000. What was the price for the whole acre?

    (A) $15,000 (B) $14,000 (C) $16,000 (D) $8,000 (E) $12,000

11. Riley's dog is 4 years older than Lara's cat. In 3 years, the sum of the ages of Riley's dog and Lara's cat will be 14. How old is Lara's cat right now?

    (A) 6 years old (B) 3 years old (C) 5 years old (D) 2 years old (E) 4 years old

12. The Venn diagram below shows the results from a recent survey. The respondents were asked whether they enjoy playing video games, reading, or both. What percentage of the survey respondents enjoy both video games and reading?

    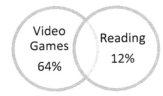

    (A) 10% (B) 15% (C) 20% (D) 24% (E) 14%

13. What is the range of the following dataset? 2753, 1584, 2349, 5012, 1307

    (A) 3057 (B) 3705 (C) 3428 (D) 1446 (E) 3075

14. A standard deck of cards is modified by adding the red queens from another deck. What is the probability that a card randomly drawn from that modified deck will be a face card (jack, queen, king)?

    (A) $\frac{8}{26}$ (B) $\frac{7}{26}$ (C) $\frac{14}{52}$ (D) $\frac{8}{27}$ (E) $\frac{7}{27}$

15. Give the slope of a line that passes through $(-7, 4)$ and $(2, 5)$.

(A) 3   (B) $\dfrac{1}{9}$ (C) $\dfrac{2}{9}$ (D) 1   (E) $\dfrac{4}{9}$

16. Give the slope of the line that passes through $(-5, 3)$ and $(1, 9)$.

(A) $\dfrac{1}{2}$ (B) $\dfrac{5}{6}$ (C) 1   (D) 2   (E) $\dfrac{1}{6}$

17. Which of the following points would be located in Quadrant III?

(A) $(-3, -2)$ (B) $(3, 2)$ (C) $(-3, 2)$ (D) $(3, -2)$ (E) $(3, 3)$

18. Simplify the expression: $2x + 15xy - 3x + 4y - 5xz + 4x$

(A) $3x + 15xy - 5xz - 4y$ (B) $3x + 15xy + 5xz + 4y$

(C) $3x + 15xy - 5xz + 4y$ (D) $3x - 15xy - 5xz + 4y$ (E) $3x - 15xy - 5xz - 4y$

19. The diameter of a circle is 16 cm. What is one-fourth of the circle's radius?

(A) 2 cm   (B) 4 cm   (C) 8 cm   (D) 1 cm   (E) 3 cm

20. What is the length of a line with endpoints $(2, 2)$ and $(10, 2)$?

(A) 2   (B) 6   (C) 12   (D) 8   (E) 9

21. A parallelogram has a base 20 cm in length, a height 16 cm in length, and a side 18 cm in length opposite the height. What is the area of the parallelogram?

(A) 350 cm   (B) 230 cm   (C) 200 cm   (D) 300 cm   (E) 320 cm

22. Find the perimeter of the given parallelogram if is height = 6, one side = 8, base = 10

(A) 20 units   (B) 60 units   (C) 30 units   (D) 90 units   (E) 15 units

23. In which quadrant or on what axis will you find the point $(-8, 12)$?

(A) quadrant I   (B) x axis   (C) quadrant II   (D) y axis   (E) quadrant III

24. The red jacks are removed from a standard deck of 52 cards. What is the probability that a card randomly drawn from that modified deck will be black?

(A) $\dfrac{13}{25}$ (B) $\dfrac{11}{25}$ (C) $\dfrac{13}{26}$ (D) $\dfrac{15}{26}$ (E) $\dfrac{21}{25}$

25. Simplify: $20x - 5(x + 8)$

(A) $15x + 40$ (B) $15x - 40$ (C) $19x + 8$ (D) $19x - 8$ (E) $25x - 40$

Answer Key

Section 1

Topic B: If I were to move to another place, I...

They say dreaming has no cost and imagination has no limits. If I were to move to another place, I would choose to be in another world where everything is free. A place where there is no concept of economy or power. People will not need to earn money for basic necessities. Nobody will try to be better than someone else because everyone is equal. There will be no war, conflict, poverty, or injustice.

Imagine a place like this. There will still be schools to learn and expand knowledge. Education will be free to all. Knowledge will be used for the betterment of the community, and nobody will be left out. Children will be taught that it is our primary responsibility to take care of our home.

Science will be focused on improving treatments for any disease, and it will be accessible to all. Preserving the world will be a priority so that the future generations may still enjoy this imaginary world.

On top of every list is ensuring no harm to the environment. Progress is relative to preserving life and the world.

Occupations will still be available, but the objective is not to earn a living. The common goal is to give back to the community. A community where everyone takes care of each other and everything in it.

There will be neither crime nor judgment. Everyone will be enjoying life as it is. People will learn that whatever we take from the world, we have to return.

What a wonderful world it would be!

Section 2

1. A	6. C	11. A	16. B	21. B
2. E	7. B	12. C	17. E	22. A
3. A	8. C	13. E	18. A	23. B
4. D	9. B	14. B	19. A	24. D
5. D	10. D	15. A	20. C	25. C

1. **Answer: A**

   The median is the middlemost value in the ordered list. Let's arrange the given list in ascending order {72, 78, 79, 80, 81, 83}. There are two numbers in the middle of the dataset—79 and 80. To get the median, we get the average of the two middle numbers: $\frac{79+80}{2} = \frac{159}{2} = 79.5$. The median of the dataset is 79.5, hence the answer is A.

2. **Answer: E**

   Range, in mathematics and statistics, is the difference between the maximum and minimum values of a dataset. The highest value in the given set is 849 and the lowest value is 245. Let's subtract the two values: 849 – 245 = 604. The range is 604, hence the answer is E.

3. **Answer: A**

   The sector in the graph representing votes for Nadia is roughly more than one-third or more than 33.33%. Among the choices, only option A has a value greater than 33.33%, hence the answer is A.

4. **Answer: D**

   A point with a positive x-coordinate and a negative y-coordinate can be found in Quadrant IV, hence the answer is D.

5. **Answer: D**

   The formula to find the area of a trapezoid is $A = \frac{1}{2}(a+b) \times h$, where a and b are the lengths of the parallel sides and h is the height. $A = \frac{1}{2}(10+20) \times 8 = \frac{1}{2}(30) \times 8 = 15 \times 8 = 120\,\text{cm}^2$. The area of the trapezoid is 120 cm², hence the answer is D.

6. **Answer: C**

   Distribute (multiply) –7 to (– 2g + 9): 14g – 63. The answer is C.

7. **Answer: B**

   First, let's make the dividend and divisor into improper fractions: $\frac{21}{5} \div \frac{28}{5}$. Next, to divide a fraction with a fraction, we need to get the reciprocal of the divisor and change the sign to multiplication: $\frac{21}{5} \times \frac{5}{28} = \frac{105}{140} = \frac{3}{4}$. The quotient is $\frac{3}{4}$, hence the answer is B.

8. **Answer: C**

   Substitute the value of C: 4(12) + 4 = 48 + 4 = 52. The answer is C.

9. **Answer: B**

   Multiply: $\frac{3}{5} \times \frac{2}{6} = \frac{6}{30} = \frac{1}{5}$. The answer is B.

10. Answer: **D**

The coat is $10 cheaper, so we can express it in a ratio of $\dfrac{10}{40}$. Divide the ratio to get the discount. $\dfrac{10}{40} = 0.25 = 25\%$. The discount is 25%, hence the answer is D.

11. Answer: **A**

Maureen needs 28 slices of pizza if she wants to give 2 slices of pizza to each of the 14 children. To get the number of pizzas she needs, divide the total number of slices she needs with the number of slices on each pizza: $28 \div 8 = 3.5$. To ensure that there will be enough pizza, round up, so Maureen needs to order 4 pizzas, hence the answer is A.

12. Answer: **C**

Multiply 420 with 20%: $420 \times \dfrac{20}{100} = 84$. 20 percent of 420 is 84, hence the answer is C.

13. Answer: **E**

We can determine whether the candidate that got the highest vote won the election outright by comparing the votes he got to the sum of the votes of his opponents. Let's add the votes won by his opponents: $2631 + 1747 + 3579 = 7957$. Delos Reyes won 8,542 votes which is more than the sum of the total of number of votes of his opponents, so we can assume that he won more than 50% of the total number of votes. Delos Reyes won the election outright, hence the answer is E.

14. Answer: **B**

Find the value of x. $5x - 42 = 53 \Rightarrow 5x = 95 \Rightarrow x = 19$. The value of x is 19, hence the answer is B.

15. Answer: **A**

Let's first distribute the "–" sign to the $(8x - 4)$. $3x + 6 - 8x + 4$. Let's then arrange the expression with like terms: $3x - 8x + 6 + 4$. Simplify: $3x - 8x + 6 + 4 = -5x + 10$. The answer is A.

16. Answer: **B**

Mean is the value obtained by dividing the sum of the data on the set with the total numbers of data on that set. $\dfrac{74 + 67 + 80 + 72 + 76 + 73 + 90 + 68}{8} = \dfrac{600}{8} = 75$. The mean is 75, hence the answer is B.

17. Answer: **E**

The median is the middlemost value in the ordered list. Let's rearrange the given list in ascending order {67, 68, 72, 73, 74, 76, 80, 90}. There are two numbers in the middle of the dataset—73 and 74. To get the median, we get the average of the two middle numbers: $\dfrac{73 + 74}{2} = \dfrac{147}{2} = 73.5$. The median of the dataset is 73.5, hence the answer is E.

18. Answer: **A**

Range, in mathematics and statistics, is the difference between the maximum and minimum values of a dataset. The highest value in the given set is 802 and the lowest value is 319. Let's subtract the two values: $802 - 319 = 483$. The range is 483, hence the answer is A.

19. Answer: **A**

Mode is the most frequently occurring value. The most frequent data on the set is 12, hence the mode is 12. The answer is A.

20. Answer: **C**

To get the length of the third leg, we can use the Pythagorean theorem since this is a right triangle. $c^2 = a^2 + b^2 \Rightarrow 10^2 = 6^2 + b^2 \Rightarrow 100 = 36 + b^2 \Rightarrow b^2 = 64 \Rightarrow b = 8$. The length of the third side is 8 ft, hence the answer is C.

21. Answer: **B**

The shaded area represents the set of all elements that are *both* in B *and not* in A. This is the intersection of B and the complement of A or $\bar{A} \cap B$, hence the answer is B.

22. Answer: **A**

For a set to be a subset of A, all of its elements must be elements of A—which means that all of its elements must be multiple of 4. If one element is not a multiple of 4, then that set cannot be a subset of A. To check which option is a subset of A, add all elements on that set and divide by four. The option with no remainder is the subset of A.

A. $12 + 16 + 20 = 48 \div 4 = 12$

B. $12 + 15 + 20 = 47 \div 4 = 11$ remainder 3

C. $8 + 12 + 14 = 34 \div 4 = 8$ remainder 2

D. $20 + 22 + 24 = 66 \div 4 = 16$ remainder 2

E. $20 + 24 + 30 = 74 \div 4 = 18$ remainder 2

Among the choices, only option A has no remainder, hence the answer is A.

23. Answer: **B**

To get the perimeter of a square, we can use the formula $P = 4s$. Since the perimeter is given, we can divide the perimeter by 4 to get the length of one side. $S = \dfrac{144}{4} = 36$. The length of one side is 36 in, hence the answer is B.

24. Answer: **D**

To get the area of triangle, we can use the formula $A = \dfrac{1}{2}bh = \dfrac{1}{2}(20 \times 15) = \dfrac{1}{2}(300) = 150$. The area of the triangle is 150 in, hence the answer is D.

25. Answer: **C**

According to the distributive property rule, for any values of a, b, c, $a(b + c) = a \times b + a \times c$. Among the choices, only option C demonstrates this rule, hence the answer is C.

Section 3

1. D	7. A	13. C	19. B	25. A	31. C	37. B
2. A	8. B	14. A	20. C	26. D	32. B	38. C
3. B	9. C	15. A	21. D	27. C	33. D	39. A
4. C	10. D	16. B	22. A	28. A	34. C	40. B
5. C	11. D	17. D	23. B	29. A	35. A	
6. A	12. B	18. C	24. D	30. B	36. C	

1. The correct answer is D. The article is about Elif Bilgin, who successfully turned banana peels into bioplastics.

2. The correct answer is A. The word "bioplastic" can be used to describe a plastic that is biodegradable, meaning it breaks down over time.

3. The correct answer is B. The article is about Elif Bilgin, who successfully turned banana peels into bioplastics.

4. The correct answer is C. Elif explained that she wanted to work with bioplastics because they could help to reduce air, land, and water pollution caused by traditional plastics, which are made with petroleum.

5. The correct answer is C. It took her 10 tries over the course of two years to make a banana-peel plastic that is sturdy and stable enough to be used in such products as artificial limbs and cable insulation.

6. The correct answer is A. Elif said she loves doing scientific research, and one of her inspirations is Marie Curie, the Nobel Prize-winning physicist who studied radioactivity.

7. The correct answer is A. Your brain forms, organizes, and stores memories in the hippocampus, which is a tiny organ that helps you form long-term memories, connect memories to other memories, and connect memories to emotions and senses.

8. The correct answer is B. The name comes from the Greek words for seahorse, because the organ is shaped kind of like one (hippo means horse and kampos means sea).

9. The correct answer is C. The hippocampus sits near the amygdala and the pineal gland, inside the temporal lobe.

10. The correct answer is D. The hippocampus can be damaged by oxygen deprivation, infection, inflammation caused by epilepsy and stress.

11. The correct answer is D. Mysterious means difficult or impossible to understand, explain, or identify.

12. The correct answer is B. Someone with a damaged hippocampus may be able to remember new things but not recall older memories, so there is a possibility to lose his/her way home or forget how to get home.

13. The correct answer is C. This tiny organ that helps you form long-term memories, connect memories to other memories, and connect memories to emotions and senses.

14. The correct answer is A. The author talks about the sisterly relationship of two Black women, which illustrates the life experiences that the women share as they grow older. From when they were younger to raising children of their own when they got older, these sisters have been inseparable.

15. The correct answer is A. The author talks about the sisterly relationship of two Black women, which illustrates the life experiences that the women share as they grow older. From when they were younger, to raising children of their own when they got older, these sisters have been inseparable. Blissful means extremely happy; full of joy, which is the most suitable answer.

16. The correct answer is B. The author talks about the inseparable bond of sisters, which illustrates the life experiences that the women share as they grow older. She talks about their bond from when they were younger to raising children of their own when they got older.

17. The correct answer is D. Purdy is the nonstandard spelling of pretty (adjective), used to represent dialect speech. All of the options are antonyms.

18. The correct answer is C. The line "coming from the same place" closely meant the same with option C. The sisters mentioned in the poem that they spent the same childhood.

19. The correct answer is B. The article talks about the heart, its chambers, and its functions. It also talks about the origin of the word "auricle."

20. The correct answer is C. Your heart is divided up into four chambers: two ventricles and two atria.

21. The correct answer is D. The auricles are floppy, wrinkled-looking pouches on either atrium, waiting to expand as blood flows into them. They got their name from the Latin word for ear.

22. The correct answer is A. The article gives information about the heart, its chambers, and its functions. It also talks about the origin of the word "auricle."

23. The correct answer is B. Floppy means tending to hang or move in a limp, loose, or ungainly way. Synonyms are flaccid, slack, and flabby.

24. The correct answer is D. The poem talks about how everything in nature depends on each other and plays an important role in making the world go around. The mountain will not be possible without the weather to form it. Without the trees on the mountains, squirrels cannot have nuts as food.

25. The correct answer is A. The poem started with the mountain and the squirrel quarrelling. Therefore, the most suitable word is "argumentative." They quarreled about how they see themselves as more important, then finally coming to an agreement that everything in nature plays a role.

26. The correct answer is D. "Latter" means denoting the second or second mentioned of two people or things. The squirrel was mentioned after the mountain in the sentence before.

27. The correct answer is C. "Latter" means denoting the second or second mentioned of two people or things. The squirrel was mentioned after the mountain in the sentence before.

28. The correct answer is A. "To crack" means to break or cause to break without a complete separation of the parts. All the other options are antonyms.

29. The correct answer is A. Neither is an adverb and is used before the first of two (or occasionally more) alternatives that are being specified (the others being introduced by "nor") to indicate that they are each untrue or do not happen.

30. The correct answer is B. The article is about returning to school soon after a concussion might be better and encouraging parents to help children socialize, not miss too much school, sleep well, and do light exercise.

31. The correct answer is C. The article shares information about how researchers think that returning to school soon after a concussion might be better.

32. The correct answer is B. Doctors recommend that parents with children who get concussions should help them socialize, not miss too much school, sleep well, and do light exercise.

33. The correct answer is D. Returning to school and daily life may help the brain recover. Research shows that children who missed less school had fewer problems after two weeks.

34. The correct answer is C. "To recover" means to return to a normal state of health, mind, or strength. Synonyms are to recuperate and heal.

35. The correct answer is A. "To socialize" means to participate in social activities; mix socially with others. Synonyms are to interact and mingle.

36. The correct answer is C. The poem is about how every little moment is something to celebrate for if we just pay attention. We don't have to wait for a big celebration for the golden moment to come.

37. The correct answer is B. The author mentioned moments that may happen to you daily that brighten your day and are moments of joy. Grateful for these moments is the most suitable description of the author's mood.

38. The correct answer is C. "To spare" means to refrain from inflicting (something) on (someone). Synonyms are to pardon and forgive.

39. The correct answer is A. "To gain" means to increase the amount or rate of (something, typically weight or speed). Synonyms are to put on and build up.

40. The correct answer is B. The article talks about little moments of joy that brighten up your day. Therefore, the most suitable answer is B.

Section 4

1. A	11. B	21. C	31. D	41. A	51. B
2. B	12. C	22. A	32. D	42. B	52. A
3. C	13. D	23. B	33. A	43. C	53. C
4. D	14. A	24. B	34. C	44. D	54. B
5. D	15. C	25. A	35. B	45. B	55. A
6. C	16. B	26. D	36. A	46. C	56. B
7. B	17. A	27. C	37. D	47. A	57. D
8. A	18. B	28. D	38. C	48. B	58. A
9. A	19. B	29. D	39. C	49. A	59. C
10. B	20. C	30. A	40. D	50. B	60. A

1. The correct answer is A. "To adapt" means to adjust to a different situation or condition. Synonyms are to acclimate, adapt, and change.

2. The correct answer is B. "To admire" means to hold in high regard. Synonyms are to adore, applaud, and appreciate.

3. The correct answer is C. "To aim" means to point or direct at a goal. Synonyms are to target, intend, and mean.

4. The correct answer is D. "To analyze" means to examine and determine. Synonyms are to evaluate, inspect, and investigate.

5.   The correct answer is D. "To assure" means to convince or relieve doubt. Synonyms are to encourage, persuade, and satisfy.

6.   The correct answer is C. "Barren" means unable to support growth. Synonyms are desolate, empty, and infertile.

7.   The correct answer is B. "To beat" means to strike (a person or an animal) repeatedly and violently so as to hurt or injure them, typically with an implement such as a club or whip. Synonyms are to hit and strike.

8.   The correct answer is A. "To compel" means to force or oblige (someone) to do something. Synonyms are to force and pressure.

9.   The correct answer is A. "To comprehend" means to grasp mentally; understand. Synonyms are to grasp and fathom.

10. The correct answer is B. A draft is a preliminary version of a piece of writing, a plan, sketch, or rough drawing. Synonyms are outline and version.

11. The correct answer is B. "Duration" means the time during which something continues. Synonyms are period and span.

12. The correct answer is C. "To debate" means to argue about (a subject), especially in a formal manner. Synonyms are to deliberate, discuss, and oppose.

13. The correct answer is D. "Eager" means (of a person's expression or tone of voice) characterized by keen expectancy or interest. Synonyms are keen and enthusiastic.

14. The correct answer is A. "Envy" is a feeling of discontented or resentful longing aroused by someone else's possessions, qualities, or luck. Synonyms are jealousy and resentment.

15. The correct answer is C. "To excavate" means to make (a hole or channel) by digging. Synonyms are to dig and burrow.

16. The correct answer is B. "Fortunate" means favored by or involving good luck or fortune; lucky.

17. The correct answer is A. "Frank" means open, honest, and direct in speech or writing, especially when dealing with unpalatable matters. Synonyms are direct and candid.

18. The correct answer is B. A gap is a break or space in an object or between two objects. Synonyms are vent and crevice.

19. The correct answer is B. "To hoard" means to amass (money or valued objects) and hide or store away. Synonyms are to store and accumulate.

20. The correct answer is C. "Homely" means (of a place or surroundings) simple but cozy and comfortable, as in one's own home. It may also mean (of a person) unattractive in appearance.

21. The correct answer is C. "To imply" means to strongly suggest the truth or existence of (something not expressly stated). Synonyms are to mean and entail.

22. The correct answer is A. "To inhabit" means to (of a person, animal, or group) live in or occupy (a place or environment).

23. The correct answer is B. "Inquiry" means an act of asking for information. It also means an official investigation. Synonyms are question and query.

24. The correct answer is B. "To judge" means to form an opinion or conclusion about. Synonyms are to conclude and deem.

25. The correct answer is A. "To justify" means to show or prove to be right or reasonable. Synonyms are to explain and defend.

26. The correct answer is D. "To keep" is to have or retain possession of. "Keep" as a noun means food, clothes, and other essentials for living.

27. The correct answer is C. "Legend" means a traditional story sometimes popularly regarded as historical but unauthenticated. It can also mean an extremely famous or notorious person, especially in a particular field.

28. The correct answer is D. "To liberate" means to set (someone) free from a situation, especially imprisonment or slavery, in which their liberty is severely restricted. Synonyms are to free and release.

29. The correct answer is D. "To lure" means to tempt (a person or animal) to do something or to go somewhere, especially by offering some form of reward. Synonyms are to tempt and entice.

30. The correct answer is A. "To meddle" means to interfere in or busy oneself unduly with something that is not one's concern.

31. The correct answer is D. The first word pair has a positive–comparative relationship. The comparative degree of good is better and of bad is worse.

32. The correct answer is D. The first word pair has an object–adjective relationship. A knife is sharp while a hammer is blunt.

33. The correct answer is A. The first word pair has a superlative–positive relationship. The superlative degree of far is farthest and of late is last (in order).

34. The correct answer is C. The first word pair has an object–adjective relationship. A child is little while a grandparent is old.

35. The correct answer is B. The first word pair has a positive–comparative relationship. The comparative degree of few is fewer and of many is more.

36. The correct answer is A. The first word pair has a positive–comparative relationship. The comparative degree of big is bigger and of little is littler (in size).

37. The correct answer is D. The first word pair has a food–food group relationship. Bacon is a source of protein while bread is a carbohydrate.

38. The correct answer is C. The first word pair has a food–food group relationship. An apple is a fruit while a broccoli is a vegetable.

39. The correct answer is C. The first word pair is antonyms. Turn on is the opposite of turn off while jump in is the opposite of jump out.

40. The correct answer is D. The first word pair is antonyms. Above is the opposite of below while front is the opposite of back.

41. The correct answer is A. The first word pair is antonyms. Absent is the opposite of present while abundant is the opposite of scarce.

42. The correct answer is B. The first word pair has a positive–comparative relationship. The comparative degree of far is further (in time) and of late is latter (in order).

43. The correct answer is C. The first word pair has a food–food group relationship. A banana is a fruit while a bean is a vegetable.

44. The correct answer is D. The first word pair has a food–food group relationship. Cold ham is a source of protein while yoghurt is a dairy product.

45. The correct answer is B. The first word pair is synonyms. Spacious is similar to wide while close is similar to shut.

46. The correct answer is C. The first word pair is synonyms. Leave is similar to abandon while hug is similar to embrace.

47. The correct answer is A. The first word pair is synonyms. Rude is similar to impolite while mad is similar to insane. Notice the addition of prefix to form the opposite word of polite and sane.

48. The correct answer is B. The first word pair is antonyms. Accept is the opposite of refuse while borrow is the opposite of lend.

49. The correct answer is A. The first word pair is synonyms. Accurate is the opposite of inaccurate while capable is the opposite of incapable. Notice the addition of prefix to form the opposite words.

50. The correct answer is B. The first word pair is antonyms. Bold is the opposite of timid while brave is the opposite of coward.

51. The correct answer is B. The first word pair has a pronoun–gender relationship. Her is a gender-specific pronoun for female while his is a gender-specific pronoun for male.

52. The correct answer is A. The first word pair has a food–time relationship. Cereal is commonly eaten for breakfast while steak is commonly eaten at dinner.

53. The correct answer is C. The first word pair has a food–time relationship. Sandwich is commonly eaten for lunch while egg is commonly eaten for breakfast.

54. The correct answer is B. The first word pair has an occupation–place of occupation relationship. A baker works at a bakery while a postman works at a post office to deliver letters or posts.

55. The correct answer is A. The first word pair has an object–state of matter relationship. The cooking oil is liquid while a ketchup bottle is solid.

56. The correct answer is B. The first word pair has an occupation–object they work on relationship. A florist designs flower arrangements while a chef cooks food.

57. The correct answer is D. The first word pair has an occupation–object they work on relationship. A hairstylist cut and styles hair while a lyricist writes lyrics to a song.

58. The correct answer is A. The first word pair has a seasonal characteristic–season relationship. There is long duration of heat in the summer while you expect to snow in the winter.

59. The correct answer is C. The first word pair has a kitchen appliance/machine–product relationship. A kettle makes hot water while a freezer makes ice cubes.

60. The correct answer is A. The first word pair has a source–product relationship. Coffee is made from beans while tea is made from leaves.

Section 5

1. B	6. B	11. D	16. C	21. E
2. A	7. A	12. D	17. A	22. B
3. D	8. E	13. B	18. C	23. C
4. E	9. A	14. E	19. A	24. A
5. C	10. C	15. B	20. D	25. B

1. Answer: **B**

    To get the perimeter of a square, we can use the formula $P = 4s$. Substitute the length of one side $P = 4s = 4(7.3) = 29.2$. The perimeter is 29.2 cm, hence the answer is B.

2. Answer: **A**

    Mean is the value obtained by dividing the sum of the data on the set with the total numbers of data on that set. $\dfrac{77+73+56+98+78+85}{6} = \dfrac{467}{6} = 77.8$. The mean is 77.8, hence the answer is A.

3. Answer: **D**

    The median is the middlemost value in the ordered list. The middle number is 12, so the median of this set is 12. The answer is D.

4. Answer: **E**

    Mode is the most frequently occurring value. Let's rearrange the given list in ascending order: 1648, 1648, 3003, 3003, 5846, 5846, 5971, 5971, 5971, 5971. The most frequent data on the set is 5971, hence the mode is 5971. The answer is E.

5. Answer: **C**

    Simplify: $5(z + 16) = 5z + 80$. The answer is C.

6. Answer: **B**

    Let's change each mixed fractions to improper fraction first, then solve.

    $$4\frac{2}{9} - 2\frac{1}{9} + 3\frac{7}{9} = \frac{38}{9} - \frac{19}{9} + \frac{34}{9} = \frac{53}{9} = 5\frac{8}{9}$$

    The answer is B.

7. Answer: **A**

Let's multiply the total price of the groceries before including the tax by the decimal equivalent of the tax rate to get the sales tax. Round it off to the nearest hundredth: 172.43 × 0.09 = 15.52. Then, add the price of the groceries to the sales tax: 172.43 + 15.52 = 187.95. The amount that needs to be paid is $187.95, hence the answer is A.

8. Answer: **E**

To divide a fraction with a fraction, we need to get the reciprocal of the divisor and change the sign to multiplication: $\frac{16}{5} \div \frac{4}{25} = \frac{16}{5} \times \frac{25}{4} = \frac{400}{20} = 20$. The quotient is 20, hence the answer is E.

9. Answer: **A**

Let x be the number. We can express the given problem with $0.25x = 340 \Rightarrow x = 1360$. 340 is 25% of 1360, hence the answer is A.

10. Answer: **C**

There are eight $\frac{1}{8}$s in a whole, so simply multiply 2,000 with 8 to get the price of the whole acre. 2000 × 8 = 16,000. The price for the whole acre is $16,000, hence the answer is C.

11. Answer: **D**

Let x be the cat's age and $x + 4$ be the dog's age. In three years, their age will be $x + 3$ and $x + 4 + 3$ or $x + 7$ respectively. It is given that in three years, the sum of their ages will be 14. Express it in an algebraic term and solve for x: $x + 3 + x + 7 = 14 \Rightarrow 2x + 10 = 14 \Rightarrow 2x = 4 \Rightarrow x = 2$. Lara's cat is currently 2 years old, hence the answer is D.

12. Answer: **D**

Let x be the percentage of the survey respondents that enjoy both playing video games and reading. The total number of survey respondents is equal to 100%. Since the common part of the Venn diagram (where A and B unite) represents the respondents that enjoy both video games and reading, we can solve for x: $100 - (64 + 12) = 24$. The percentage of the survey respondents that enjoy both playing video games and reading is 24%, hence the answer is D.

13. Answer: **B**

Range, in mathematics and statistics, is the difference between the maximum and minimum values of a dataset. The highest value in the given set is 5012 and the lowest value is 1307. Let's subtract the two values: 5012 − 1307 = 3705. The range is 3705, hence the answer is B.

14. Answer: **E**

There are twelve face cards in a standard deck (4 jacks, 4 queens, and 4 kings). If we will add two red queens, it will now be 14 face cards out of 54 cards (there are 52 cards in a standard deck, adding the two red queens, we will have 54 cards). The probability of getting a face card in this modified deck will be $\frac{14}{54}$ or $\frac{7}{27}$, hence the answer is E.

15. **Answer: B**

    To get the slope, we can use the formula $m = \dfrac{y_2 - y_1}{x_2 - x_1} = \dfrac{5 - 4}{2 - (-7)} = \dfrac{1}{9}$. The slope is $\dfrac{1}{9}$, so the answer is B.

16. **Answer: C**

    To get the slope, we can use the formula $m = \dfrac{y_2 - y_1}{x_2 - x_1} = \dfrac{9 - 3}{1 - (-5)} = \dfrac{6}{6} = 1$. The slope is 1, hence the answer is C.

17. **Answer: A**

    By definition, a point on the coordinate plane that is in Quadrant III must have both negative x-coordinate and negative y-coordinate. Among the choices, only option A satisfies both conditions, hence the answer is A.

18. **Answer: C**

    Arrange the expression with like terms: $2x - 3x + 4x + 15xy - 5xz + 4y$. Simplify the like terms: $2x - 3x + 4x + 15xy - 5xz + 4y = 3x + 15xy - 5xz + 4y$. The answer is C.

19. **Answer: A**

    Radius is one-half of a circle's diameter. The given diameter is 16 cm, so one-half of it will be 8 cm, which is the length of the radius. To get the one-fourth of the radius, simply divide it by 4: $8 \div 4 = 2$. The one-fourth of the radius is 2 cm, hence the answer is A.

20. **Answer: D**

    To find the length of the line, you can simply subtract 10 from 2: $10 - 2 = 8$. Since the y-coordinates are the same, we don't have to take any vertical direction into account. The length of the line is 8, hence the answer is D.

21. **Answer: E**

    To get the area of a parallelogram, we can use the formula $A = b \times h = 20 \times 16 = 320$. The area of the parallelogram is 320 cm, hence the answer is E.

22. **Answer: B**

    To get the area of a parallelogram, we can use the formula $A = b \times h = 6 \times 10 = 60$. The area of the parallelogram is 60 units, hence the answer is B.

23. **Answer: C**

    The point $(-8, 12)$ has a negative x-coordinate and a positive y-coordinate. By definition, any point on a coordinate plane that satisfies these conditions is located in Quadrant II, hence the answer is C.

24. Answer: **A**

    There are 52 cards in a standard deck. If we remove 2 red jacks, we will now have 50 cards left. The probability of getting a black card in this modified deck will be $\dfrac{26}{50}$ or $\dfrac{13}{25}$, hence the answer is A.

25. Answer: **B**

    Simplify: $20x - 5(x + 8) = 20x - 5x - 40 = 15x - 40$. The answer is B.

SSAT Middle Level Exam 2

SECTION 1

WRITING SAMPLE

Time—25 minutes

Directions:

Read the following topics carefully. Take a few minutes to select the topic you find more interesting. Think about the topic and organize your thoughts on a scrap paper before you begin writing.

Topic A: If I were to choose between...

Topic B: This holiday, I...

Circle your selection: Topic A or Topic B. Write your essay for the selected topic on the paper provided. Your essay should NOT exceed two pages and must be written in pencil. Be sure that your handwriting is legible and that you must stay within the lines and margins.

SECTION 2

QUANTITATIVE MATH

Time—30 minutes

25 Questions

In this section, there are five possible answers after each problem. Choose which one is best.

Example

$5,413 - 4,827 =$

(A) 586
(B) 596
(C) 696
(D) 1,586
(E) 1,696

Answer

● Ⓑ Ⓒ Ⓓ Ⓔ

The correct answer to this question is lettered A, so space A is marked.

---

1. Simplify: $37x - (24x - 15y) + 29y$

(A) $13x + 34y$ (B) $13x - 14y$ (C) $13x + 14y$ (D) $13x - 44y$ (E) $13x + 44y$

2. Define sets K and L as follows: $K = \{x | x$ is a multiple of 5$\}$ and $L = \{295, 374, 168, 725, 560, 927\}$. How many elements are in the set K∩L?

(A) 2 (B) 5 (C) 3 (D) 4 (E) cannot be determined

3. Find the slope of a line with points $(-7,1)$ and $(-2,5)$.

(A) $\frac{4}{5}$ (B) $-\frac{4}{5}$ (C) $-\frac{2}{5}$ (D) $\frac{1}{5}$ (E) $-\frac{4}{9}$

4. Cleo recently put a rectangular fence around her backyard. The fence has a width of 12 yd and a length of 16 yd. If Cleo paid $11.75 for every yard of fence, how much did the fence cost?

(A) $865 (B) $586 (C) $658 (D) $685 (E) $568

5. The coordinates of A and D are A(5,2) and D(8,0). Find the length of the diagonal of the following rectangle:

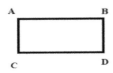

(A) 3.6 u   (B) 2.7 u   (C) 3.1 u   (D) 2.9 u   (E) 2.6 u

6. Montclair High conducted a standardized test for its students. The table below gives the number of students who scored in each of the five ranges.

Score	Students
91–100	18
81–90	49
71–80	67
61–70	54
51–60	12

No student scored below 51. What percent of the students score 70 or less (nearest whole percent)?

(A) 25%   (B) 42%   (C) 50%   (D) 33%   (E) 44%

7. Find the area of a parallelogram with a height of 10 cm, base of 8 cm, and a side length of 6 cm.

(A) 58 cm²   (B) 48 cm²   (C) 60 cm²   (D) 80 cm²   (E) 90 cm²

8. Simplify: $\dfrac{11}{15} + \dfrac{7}{15} - \dfrac{12}{15}$

(A) $\dfrac{2}{5}$ (B) $\dfrac{3}{5}$ (C) $\dfrac{1}{5}$ (D) $\dfrac{4}{5}$ (E) $\dfrac{2}{3}$

9. 88 is what percent of 400?

(A) 20%   (B) 27%   (C) 21%   (D) 25%   (E) 22%

10. Chris earns $10.00 for each hour he works. For every hour he works, he then gives $2.00 to his sister Kayla. How much money will Kayla have if Chris works 14.5 hours?

(A) $29.50   (B) $29.00   (C) $28.00   (D) $30.00   (E) $15.00

11. The square root of a number is 43. What is that number?

(A) 1894   (B) 1498   (C) 1849   (D) 1489   (E) 1948

12. Which of the following numbers is divisible by 9 without a remainder?

(A) 539   (B) 540   (C) 537   (D) 533   (E) 542

13. It took Neil 15 minutes to walk 3 km. If he walks for 6 km more at the same speed, what part of an hour will his entire 9km walk take?

(A) $\dfrac{1}{2}$ (B) $\dfrac{1}{3}$ (C) $\dfrac{2}{3}$ (D) $\dfrac{3}{5}$ (E) $\dfrac{3}{4}$

14. If Liam cooks one-third of half a dozen eggs, how many eggs has he cooked?

(A) 2   (B) 4   (C) 1   (D) 6   (E) 3

15. The perimeter of an equilateral triangle ABC is 4 times the perimeter of equilateral triangle XYZ. If the perimeter of ABC is 36 m, what is the length of one side of XYZ?

(A) 4 m   (B) 8 m   (C) 3 m   (D) 9 m   (E) 5 m

16. 20 colored dice are placed in a hat—10 red, 4 blue, 6 yellow. What is the probability that a randomly drawn dice will not be blue?

(A) 70%   (B) 80%   (C) 60%   (D) 75%   (E) 90%

17. Find the perimeter of a trapezoid if the dimensions are $s_1 = 5$, $b_1 = 4$, $b_2 = 6$, $s_2 = 6$.

(A) 20 u   (B) 22 u   (C) 18 u   (D) 21 u   (E) 25 u

18. The ratio of doctors to nurses in the hospital with a staff of 121 is 4 to 7. How many more nurses than doctors are there?

(A) 36   (B) 38   (C) 30   (D) 35   (E) 33

19. Complete the set by determining the value of a. {1, 4, 9, 16, 25, 36, 49, a}

(A) 56   (B) 54   (C) 65   (D) 64   (E) 66

20. What is the mode of this set: 458, 967, 127, 567, 458, 678, 458, 127, 967, 458

(A) 458   (B) 127   (C) 678   (D) 967   (E) 567

21. Find the median of the set: 12, 56, 18, 64, 29, 30, 74, 24, 33

(A) 30   (B) 56   (C) 64   (D) 33   (E) 29

22. Simplify: $(4x - 5x + 2) - (3x + 1)$

(A) $4x - 1$ (B) $4x + 1$ (C) $-4x + 1$ (D) $-4x - 1$ (E) $-4x + 2$

23. Given that $x = 5$, $y = 3$, $z = 8$, find the product of xyz.

(A) 80 (B) 120 (C) 60 (D) 40 (E) 100

24. The triangle below has an area of 450 in². If $x = 20$ in, then what is the value of y?

(A) 54 in (B) 45 in (C) 90 in (D) 60 in (E) 75 in

25. For a party, Clint brought 4 boxes of cookies, each containing 10 cookies. He gave each of his friends 3 cookies, and then he eats 6 cookies himself. He now has 4 cookies left. How many friends did Clint give cookies to?

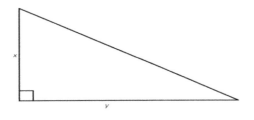

(A) 18 (B) 11 (C) 10 (D) 12 (E) 15

SECTION 3

READING COMPREHENSION

Time—40 minutes
40 Questions

Read each passage carefully and then answer the questions about it. For each question, decide on the basis of the passage which one of the choices best answers the question.

Water is precious at certain seasons in Egypt, for there it almost never rains. The sky is blue and cloudless, and the sun shines steadily on, day after day. The people often sleep on the flat roofs of their houses. So, if we, being tired and warm, should stop at a coffee house to rest, we should very likely find that it consisted merely of a roof to keep off the sun's rays, and a number of willow benches. On these benches would be seated grave looking men in turbans and loose robes, and on the floor about, numbers of peasants would be seated cross-legged. Each man would probably have in one hand a cup of coffee and in the other, a long pipe. The coffee they bring us is thick, muddy liquid, and has in it neither sugar nor milk. They would not know what to think of us, if we should ask for milk, for they never heard of its being used in coffee, and an order for sugar would throw the proprietor into great confusion. He would probably have to send to the market for a lump. But though it has no sugar and milk, the coffee is very fragrant, for the berry is crushed, instead of being <u>ground</u>.

From A Christmas at School *by Dodd, Mead & Company*

1. Where is the setting of the story?

   (A) Egypt   (B) an unknown country in the Middle East   (C) South Africa   (D) Bahamas

2. After reading the sentence "The sky is blue and cloudless, and the sun shines steadily on, day after day," we can assume that the weather is?

   (A) foggy   (B) hot   (C) stormy   (D) freezing

3. Why will the people react differently if someone asks for milk and sugar on their coffee in the story?

   (A) they do not have milk

   (B) milk is expensive

   (C) for they never heard of it being used in coffee

   (D) milk is banned in their country

4. What makes their coffee very fragrant?

(A) due to the type of land they grow their coffee in

(B) because they put aromatics to the coffee

(C) for they use a different source to make coffee

(D) for the berry is crushed instead of being ground

5. Which among the words used in the story is an adjective?

(A) sleep   (B) often   (C) and   (D) muddy

6. What is the meaning of the word "ground" as used in the story?

(A) solid surface of the earth

(B) to place on a foundation

(C) reduced to fine particles

(D) to furnish with a ground

Maya's campaign has two goals: to raise awareness about and to push plastic stickers to be banned. Kids are asked to share their own sticker collections with their local MP by May 7.

The campaign is a call to Environment and Climate Change Minister Steven Guilbeault to expand Canada's new single-use plastic ban to include stickers on fruits and vegetables.

Maya said she hopes to inspire kids and adults to act. "Maybe seeing a child doing this can inspire others to do the same." Maya said even if kids don't want to "get political" and send the stickers to their MPs, she hopes they'll at least start disposing of the stickers properly.

Plastic PLU stickers are used by the produce industry to label bulk fruits and vegetables that are sold loose at the grocery store. The stickers are used around the world to make sure customers are paying the right price for an item and to prevent items from getting mixed up, said Jane Proctor, vice-president of the Canadian Produce Marketing Association (CPMA). Most PLU stickers are made from plastic, ink and adhesive (sticky stuff). If PLU stickers made of plastic are banned, Proctor said they would have to be replaced with a substitute. PLU stickers can be made of paper and other compostable materials, but Proctor said it's "a durability issue," meaning they have to be able to stay on the items while travelling to the store and on the shelves. Plastic is currently the most durable material, she said. One of the main issues with most plastic stickers is that they don't break down in the compost. If you use that compost in your backyard, it can contaminate the soil and can end up in waterways, such as rivers and lakes. It also means organic (green bin) waste collected by towns and cities that is contaminated by stickers can get diverted away from composting facilities and instead sent straight to the regular landfill. That's a problem, according to the FOE, because the fruits and veggies will break down and create methane, a greenhouse gas that contributes to climate change. Maya said that while she hopes for a ban, awareness is the larger goal.

"Even if we don't get our end result, banning them in Canada, at least people will be aware not to put them in their compost."

From Why this 10-year-old is raising awareness about plastic produce stickers *by CBC Kids News*

7. What is the article mainly about?

    (A) about how durable plastic stickers are

    (B) about Maya's campaign on raising awareness about plastic produce stickers

    (C) about ineffective composting

    (D) about the available replacements for plastic stickers

8. What are the objectives of Maya's campaign?

    (A) to raise awareness about plastic stickers

    (B) to push plastic stickers to be banned

    (C) both A and B

    (D) neither A nor B

9. Why are plastic stickers on fruits and veggies requested to be included in the single-use plastic ban?

    (A) they are impractical

    (B) they produce carbon monoxide which harms the ozone

    (C) they are ugly to look at and sticky even when wet

    (D) plastic stickers don't break down and, if added to compost, will contaminate the soil

10. What is the current challenge in banning plastic stickers?

    (A) durability issue

    (B) not eye-catching to consumers

    (C) replacements cannot be color coded

    (D) replacements are more expensive

11. Why are plastic stickers preferred?

    (A) they are cheap

    (B) they are easy to find

    (C) plastic is currently the most durable material

    (D) they are pleasing to the consumers' eyes

12. What is the use of plastic stickers?

(A) to label bulk fruits and vegetables that are sold loose at the grocery store

(B) to make sure customers are paying the right price for an item

(C) to prevent items from getting mixed up

(D) all of the above

13. We can assume that the only way for the plastic stickers be included in the single-use plastic ban is?

(A) to wage a war against the PLU industry

(B) to run a protest and get more participants

(C) to find a replacement as durable as the PLU but break down in the compost

(D) to stop buying produce from the grocery store

While he was singing, two children, hearing him, came close up behind him, and when he had finished began to cough in order to attract his attention. For some time, he took no notice, but at last he turned, and he saw two nicely-dressed children, a little boy and a girl, who wished him good evening and made a bow. He was about to speak to them, when their father, who had also heard him singing, came up, and <u>supposing</u> him to be an Englishman, said to him in English, "Although, sir, we are strangers, it is true, those beautiful words you were singing, which I am sure come from your heart, prove to me that both look up to one common Father in heaven. I am the pastor of the little village you can see down there, at the foot of the mountain. But it is growing dark, and if, as I presume, you are a stranger in these parts, I can gladly offer you the simple accommodation of my cottage for the night."

From Captain's Story *by William S. Martin (Author)*

14. After reading the story, we can assume that the pastor is?

(A) kind (B) proud (C) intelligent (D) strong

15. What is implied by the phrase "it is growing dark"?

(A) an eclipse (B) almost nighttime (C) noon time (D) stormy clouds coming

16. What does the phrase "come from your heart" mean?

(A) breathing heavily (B) sincere (C) singing from the diaphragm (D) romantic

17. Which of the words used in the story is a verb?

(A) look up (B) nicely-dressed (C) him (D) although

18. What does the underlined word "supposing" mean?

(A) proving right

(B) setting someone last

(C) rejecting someone's presence

(D) assuming something of the subject

The ozone is a see-through layer that surrounds the Earth that keeps the sun's strong, harmful rays from burning us.

Since the 1980s, scientists around the world have been worried because the ozone was disappearing.

But new research from the U.S. National Oceanic and Atmospheric Administration, published on Aug. 24, 2022, is suggesting we may nearly be in the clear.

That's because a lot of the harmful chemicals that were destroying it have been banned.

CBC Kids News asked Tara Ivanochko, an environmental scientist and University of British Columbia professor, to break down the new research.

Q: What was the concern with the ozone?

A: For a period of time, we were using chemicals for things like refrigerants [a chemical used to make things cool] that would get released into the atmosphere and break down the ozone. More ultraviolet light [from the sun] was able to penetrate through and we were seeing impacts here on Earth, like higher UV indexes.

With the way the atmosphere circulates, many chemicals will concentrate in the polar areas of Earth. So, ozone holes started to develop in those areas, especially over Antarctica. However, they weren't holes exactly, but less concentration of ozone in the polar regions, rather.

Q: Oh no! What was done to help our beloved ozone?

A: It became evident that this was a global problem because it had to do with the use of these chemicals all around the world. So, there was an international agreement around the problem and solution. That agreement was called the Montreal protocol, held here in Canada in 1987. Scientists identified certain chemicals that were agreed upon to remove from production.

From Fewer chemicals is good news for Earth's ozone. Here's why *by CBC Kids News*

19. What is the article about?

(A) the history of the international agreement

(B) the history of ozone depletion

(C) the great scientists who researched on the cause of the ozone depletion

(D) the current status of the ozone, the problem before, and solution that helped clear the problem

20. What chemicals were banned in the international agreement that helped in the ozone recovery?

(A) plastic stickers (B) plastic straws (C) plastic planters (D) refrigerants

21. When and where was the international agreement held?

(A) in Canada in 1987

(B) in Canada in 1978

(C) in South America in 1987

(D) in California in 1987

22. What is the ozone?

(A) a chemical used to make things cool

(B) an international agreement banning certain chemicals in production

(C) a see-through layer that surrounds the Earth that keeps the sun's strong, harmful rays from burning us

(D) ultraviolet light from the sun

23. Why did ozone holes start to develop in the polar regions?

(A) due to the revolution of the Earth around the moon

(B) with the way the atmosphere circulates, many chemicals will concentrate in the polar areas

(C) due to the tidal waves

(D) because of the storms

Near the sheet of water there was a large and beautiful farm belonging to Adalbert's parents: a dozen cows in a long barn, besides a bull, which caused fear merely by a glance of his very mild eyes; farther off a large stable occupied by seven or eight tall and robust working horses; in front, four hundred sheep crowded one against another, living happily, gentle as lambs. In the barn-yard, in the barn, in the stable, upon the manure heap, under the shed, everywhere, hens, chickens, cockerels, geese, ducks, a whole community of little beings, fluttered around, laid eggs, bathed, fought, and scorned the world in an incredible manner.

Mother Barru was the queen of this peaceable empire. She was a woman of good sense, and her good humor <u>ceased</u> only on two occasions—when a boy on the farm got drunk, and when a hen hid her eggs at a distance.

From House on wheels *by Stolz (Author)*

24. Which feeling best describes what the short story implies?

(A) blissful (B) miserable (C) upset (D) ungrateful

25. After reading the short story, we may presume that the setting is?

(A) by the countryside (B) in the metro city (C) in a tropical island (D) in a vast desert

26. Who owns the area in the short story?

(A) it was an inherited by Adalbert

(B) Adalbert's parents

(C) Adalbert's cousin

(D) the town's priest

27. What is the meaning of the word "cease"?

(A) to proceed to perform the first or earliest part of some action

(B) to start again

(C) to come to an end

(D) to persist in anything undertaken

28. Which of the words used in the short story is a noun?

(A) near   (B) was   (C) beside   (D) fear

29. When did Mother Barru get angry?

(A) when a boy on the farm got drunk

(B) when a hen hid her eggs at a distance

(C) never, she was a woman of good sense

(D) both A and B

Everyone can agree that governments are morally obligated to protect their citizens. But what if countries were also held legally responsible for protecting present and future generations from the climate crisis?

Recently, Vanuatu, a tiny Pacific Island nation with a population of just 320,000, proposed a resolution on climate justice at the United Nations General Assembly Meeting.

The new resolution calls upon the International Court of Justice (ICJ) to issue an advisory opinion on nations that don't meet their climate obligations. The resolution passed with the support of a core group of 17 nations and 132 co-sponsoring nations.

Although not legally binding, this could *propel* the climate justice movement forward and serve as a huge victory for smaller nations.

From A Big Win For A Small Island Nation *by Ritali J, Writer Intern, youngzine*

30. What is the main topic of the article?

(A) about the United Nations

(B) about the population of Vanuatu

(C) about the proposed resolution on climate justice to make countries morally obligated to protect their citizens

(D) about the number of nations involved in the United Nations

31. Which best describes the article?

(A) emotional   (B) informative   (C) argumentative   (D) melancholic

32. What is the goal of the proposed resolution on climate justice?

(A) to pass a law to arrest those who do not segregate their garbage properly

(B) to promote reusable plastic bags when shopping

(C) to issue an advisory opinion on nations that don't meet their climate obligations

(D) to mandate recycling day to be every Wednesday of the week

33. How many people are inhabiting Vanuatu?

(A) 132   (B) 17   (C) 32,000   (D) 320,000

34. Which of the words used in the article is an adjective?

(A) advisory   (B) opinion   (C) morally   (D) obligated

35. What does the underlined word "propel" mean?

(A) to draw or haul toward oneself or itself

(B) to obstruct by opposition or difficulty

(C) move forward or onward

(D) to set aside; reserve

Many climate activists are frustrated with the lack of action by governments to stop burning fossil fuels and address the climate crisis. Their goal was simple: to spark an emotional reaction.

According to Anna Holland, an activist, she would like to see people extend the protectiveness they feel towards a famous painting to life on Earth.

Last Generation, an organization whose protestors threw mashed potatoes at Monet's painting, Grainstacks, in Germany, has demanded a 62-mile-per-hour speed limit on German highways. This would save 5.4 million tons of carbon dioxide per year. Additionally, they claim that a flat-fee ticket for railroad trains will decrease emissions by encouraging the use of public transit.

This is not the first-time protestors have targeted art before. Nearly a century ago, suffragists attacked the painting The Toiled of Venus, and experienced <u>backlash</u> from the press.

From Should Art Be Held Hostage? by Shreeya G, Writer Intern, youngzine

36. Why do activists target famous paintings?

    (A) for power

    (B) to spark an emotional reaction

    (C) to stop putting importance on paintings

    (D) to discourage people from pursuing art

37. Why did protestors demand a 62-mile-per-hour speed limit on German highways?

    (A) to avoid accidents with pedestrians

    (B) to prevent vehicular collision

    (C) save 5.4 million tons of carbon dioxide per year

    (D) so that passengers can enjoy the view while traveling

38. What is the objective of the article ?

    (A) to enlighten   (B) to discourage   (C) to promote   (D) to resent

39. Which is a synonym of the word "backlash"?

    (A) splatter of water   (B) resistance   (C) background   (D) dodge

40. Which word used in the article is a preposition?

    (A) has   (B) toward   (C) she   (D) threw

SECTION 4

VERBAL REASONING

Time—30 minutes
60 Questions

This section consists of two different types of questions. There are directions for each type.

Each of the following questions consists of one word followed by four words or phrases. You have to select a word or phrase whose meaning is closest to the word in capital letters.

Example

SWIFT: (A) clean   (B) fancy   (C) fast   (D) quiet

Answer

(A)(B)●(D)

1. SUDDEN

   (A) delayed   (B) lazy   (C) gradual   (D) unexpected

2. ADJUST

   (A) modify   (B) adore   (C) denounce   (D) hate

3. WORRIED

   (A) ignore   (B) concerned   (C) calm   (D) happy

4. PRODUCTIVE

   (A) idle   (B) inactive   (C) fruitful   (D) weak

5. BOAST

   (A) conceal   (B) hide   (C) brag   (D) fail

6. UNPREDICTABLE

   (A) uncertain   (B) certain   (C) dependable   (D) definite

7. BRIEF

   (A) lengthy   (B) long   (C) slow   (D) quick

8. DOUBTFUL

(A) unclear (B) clear (C) secure (D) sure

9. ECONOMICAL

(A) careless (B) practical (C) expensive (D) wasteful

10. ATTEMPT

(A) forget (B) neglect (C) try (D) overlook

11. HESITATE

(A) pause (B) continue (C) persist (D) agree

12. THRIVE

(A) cease (B) grow (C) fail (D) halt

13. PLEASING

(A) bitter (B) boring (C) delightful (D) disagreeable

14. RANDOM

(A) planned (B) systematic (C) specific (D) irregular

15. OVERWHELM

(A) comfort (B) aid (C) assist (D) overpower

16. NOBLE

(A) bad (B) dignified (C) common (D) modest

17. ATTRACT

(A) entice (B) bore (C) disgust (D) repel

18. IMITATE

(A) differ (B) mimic (C) original (D) oppose

19. DEFINITE

(A) doubtful (B) vague (C) exact (D) unclear

20. FAMOUS

(A) common   (B) ordinary   (C) typical   (D) renowned

21. DIFFICULT

(A) easy   (B) effortless   (C) hard   (D) simple

22. HONOR

(A) commemorate   (B) blame   (C) condemn   (D) disregard

23. FAITHFUL

(A) devoted   (B) cold   (C) corrupt   (D) negligent

24. OBVIOUS

(A) concealed   (B) evident   (C) dark   (D) hidden

25. IMMEDIATELY

(A) later   (B) eventually   (C) never   (D) instantly

26. DESIRE

(A) dislike   (B) hate   (C) crave   (D) despise

27. CEASE

(A) begin   (B) complete   (C) discontinue   (D) persevere

28. DISGUST

(A) distaste   (B) approval   (C) liking   (D) admiration

29. BREACH

(A) rift   (B) closure   (C) bridge   (D) agreement

30. SUITABLE

(A) awkward   (B) fitting   (C) improper   (D) inappropriate

The following questions ask you to find the relationships between words. For each question, select the choice that best completes the meaning of the sentence.

Example	Answer
Ann carried the box carefully so that she would not _____ the pretty glasses.	●Ⓑ©Ⓓ
(A) break (B) fix (C) open (D) stop	

31. Winter is to sweater as summer is to

    (A) August (B) hat (C) hot (D) sun

32. Tea is to teacup as ice-cream is to

    (A) melt (B) vanilla (C) cone (D) soft

33. Comb is to hair as slippers is to

    (A) new (B) red (C) rubber (D) feet

34. Hot is to sweat as cold is to

    (A) shiver (B) age (C) grandparent (D) young

35. Bird is to sky as fish is to

    (A) fried (B) sea (C) mackerel (D) swim

36. Sun is to morning as moon is to

    (A) outer space (B) star (C) crater (D) night

37. Dark is to light as hot is to

    (A) coffee (B) cold (C) sun (D) day

38. Open is to close as free is to

    (A) cage (B) liberty (C) captive (D) sample

39. Happy is to sad as beautiful in is to

    (A) pretty (B) girl (C) adjective (D) ugly

40. Clever is to dumb as wise is to

    (A) ignorant (B) old (C) teacher (D) smart

41. King is to queen as duke is to

    (A) palace (B) duchess (C) monarch (D) male

42. Doctor is to hospital and chef is to

    (A) restaurant (B) apron (C) cook (D) food

43. Pen is to write as camera is to

    (A) film (B) flash (C) capture (D) photography

44. Chair is to sit as bed is to

    (A) mattress (B) sleep (C) headboard (D) bedroom

45. Squirrel is to acorn as rabbit is to

    (A) carrots (B) fur (C) hare (D) hop

46. Teacher is to student as parent is to

    (A) adults (B) children (C) family (D) discipline

47. Clock is to time as thermometer is to

    (A) armpit (B) mercury (C) glass (D) temperature

48. Plane is to fly as ship is to

    (A) sail (B) steel (C) ocean (D) captain

49. Numbers is to count as words is to

    (A) paper (B) alphabet (C) read (D) book

50. Crew is to sailors as company is to

    (A) soldiers (B) friend (C) noun (D) business

51. Ladder is to climb as needle to

    (A) sew (B) sharp (C) thread (D) clothing

52. Laugh is to happy as cry is to

(A) cheerful (B) sad (C) tears (D) eyes

53. Quiet is to noisy as silent is to

(A) library (B) timid (C) loud (D) mouth

54. Strawberry is to jam as milk is to

(A) cow (B) drink (C) liquid (D) cheese

55. Death is to mourning as birth is to

(A) cake (B) celebration (C) hospital (D) mother

56. Red is to primary as green is to

(A) leaves (B) nature (C) secondary (D) color

57. Admire is to adore as adapt is to

(A) conform (B) neglect (C) reject (D) new

58. Agile is to lively as sluggish is to

(A) active (B) inactive (C) worker (D) adjective

59. Ambiguous is to unclear as precise is to

(A) definite (B) shot (C) guess (D) vague

60. Earphones is to ears as keyboard is to

(A) computer (B) fingers (C) electronics (D) mechanical

SECTION 5

QUANTITATIVE MATH

Time—30 minutes

25 Questions

In this section, there are five possible answers after each problem. Choose which one is best.

Example

$5{,}413 - 4{,}827 =$

(A) 586
(B) 596
(C) 696
(D) 1,586
(E) 1,686

Answer

● Ⓑ Ⓒ Ⓓ Ⓔ

The correct answer to this question is lettered A, so space A is marked.

---

1. Express the following ratio in simplest form: 210:90

    (A) 7:3 (B) 8:1 (C) 7:2 (D) 8:3 (E) 7:4

2. What is the value of x in $\dfrac{x}{x+3} = \dfrac{4}{7}$?

    (A) 3 (B) 4 (C) 2 (D) 5 (E) 1

3. 324 is 30% of what number?

    (A) 1880 (B) 1008 (C) 1088 (D) 1800 (E) 1080

4. Simplify: $\dfrac{11}{15} - \dfrac{3}{5}$

    (A) $\dfrac{3}{15}$ (B) $\dfrac{2}{15}$ (C) $\dfrac{7}{15}$ (D) $\dfrac{4}{15}$ (E) $\dfrac{11}{15}$

5. Find the perimeter of a triangle with sides 8 cm, 9 cm, and 10 cm.

    (A) 1 (B) 27 cm (C) 27 cm (D) 23 cm (E) 29 cm

6. A square has sides measuring 5 in. What is this square's perimeter?

    (A) 15 in (B) 16 in (C) 20 in² (D) 20 in (E) 10 in

7. What would be the area of a parallelogram if the height is 9 cm, the base is 8 cm, and one of the side length is 7 cm.

(A) 75 in²   (B) 70 in²   (C) 72 in²   (D) 62 in²   (E) 82 in²

8. Find the length of the line segment whose endpoints are (–2, 4) and (3, 2).

(A) 5.39 u   (B) 5.93 u   (C) 3.39 u   (D) 3.59 u   (E) 3.93 u

9. In which quadrant or on which axis will you find the point (–5, –9)?

(A) quadrant I   (B) x-axis   (C) y-axis   (D) quadrant II   (E) quadrant III

10. Give the slope of a line that passes through (4, 5) and (2, 3).

(A) 2.5   (B) 3   (C) 5   (D) 2   (E) 1

For questions 11 and 12, refer to the table below: Carla's and Luis's TV viewing hours is closely being monitored by their mother. The table below shows the number of hours of TV viewing for a week.

Days	Carla	Luis
Sunday	4.2	3.9
Monday	1.2	1.5
Tuesday	1.6	1.4
Wednesday	1.3	1.3
Thursday	1.5	1.5
Friday	1.1	1.3
Saturday	3.6	3.5

11. On which day of the week is the combined total of Carla's and Luis's TV viewing the highest?

(A) Saturday   (B) Monday   (C) Friday   (D) Sunday   (E) Wednesday

12. On which day of the week is the combined total of Carla's and Luis's TV viewing the lowest?

(A) Saturday   (B) Monday   (C) Friday   (D) Sunday   (E) Wednesday

13. Barbara took five tests and quizzes this semester. If her grades were 94, 90, 91, 92, and 95, what is her median test score?

(A) 95   (B) 92   (C) 91   (D) 94   (E) 90

14. Find the mean of this set of numbers: 421, 563, 398, 236, 107

(A) 354   (B) 345   (C) 340   (D) 435   (E) 453

15. Multiply: $6b \times 12b$

(A) $72b^2$ (B) $75b^2$ (C) $72b$ (D) $66b^2$ (E) $60b^2$

16. 20 added to one-fourth of a number is equal to 56. What is the number?

(A) 1   (B) 16   (C) 20   (D) 20   (E) 10

17. Which of the following is a subset of the set: $A = \{x | x$ is a prime number$\}$?

(A) $\{3, 5, 21, 30\}$ (B) $\{7, 9, 11, 12\}$ (C) $\{3, 7, 11, 13\}$ (D) $\{5, 11, 13, 15\}$ (E) $\{23, 27, 29, 30\}$

18. Find the slope of the line that passes through the points $(5, -4)$ and $(-3, -6)$.

(A) $\dfrac{1}{2}$ (B) $\dfrac{5}{8}$ (C) $\dfrac{3}{8}$ (D) $\dfrac{3}{4}$ (E) $\dfrac{1}{4}$

19. A square has an area of 121 sq units, what is the perimeter of the square?

(A) 34 u   (B) 45 u   (C) 40 u   (D) 44 u   (E) 22 u

20. Solve: $\dfrac{4}{5} \div \dfrac{5}{6}$

(A) $\dfrac{17}{25}$ (B) $\dfrac{21}{25}$ (C) $\dfrac{24}{25}$ (D) $\dfrac{23}{25}$ (E) $\dfrac{19}{25}$

21. A class with 30 students went on a field trip, but three of the students were absent. What percentage of students in the class went on the field trip?

(A) 90%   (B) 92%   (C) 95%   (D) 93%   (E) 91.5%

22. What is the perimeter of an equilateral triangle with a side length 4 in?

(A) 11 in   (B) 12 in   (C) 15 in   (D) 20 in   (E) 10 in

23. The width of a rectangle is $3x$, the length is $6x$, and the perimeter is 72. What is the value of x?

(A) 4   (B) 8   (C) 6   (D) 2   (E) 18

24. In which quadrant or on which axis will you find the point $(0,5)$?

(A) x-axis   (B) quadrant I   (C) y-axis   (D) quadrant II   (E) quadrant IV

25. Find the range of this set of numbers: 48, 34, 95, 67, 50, 42, 81

(A) 57   (B) 61   (C) 34   (D) 50   (E) 48

Answer Key

Section 1

Topic B: If I were to choose between…

Every day we make choices. They may be for us or in consideration of someone important to us.

If I were to choose between living one life and being immortal, I would still choose to live one life and eventually meet death. I would love to live a long life and not perish soon but the thought of immortality is scary. At first thought, it may seem a good idea to be immortal. Imagine the things you could accomplish if you could live forever. There will no shortage of time. You will never find yourself rushing in the morning to have everything completed in a day because you know that many tomorrows will come. Why is it scary, you may ask.

Imagine to outlive everyone. You will witness every loved one's loss and you'll always be the one left in sorrow. You will carry the grief all those years which will not end. The thought of having unlimited tomorrows will not give you a sense of accountability to accomplish anything because it will not matter when you'll start doing them. You will always wake up to a new day and live through who knows how many decades. Time will come there will be nothing that will inspire you to get up and do something. You will lose the essence of living. The fact that all of us return to dust makes us be determined to live our lives to the fullest. When you are not sure that there will be tomorrow, every day will be a day you cherish. Isn't that a wonderful way to live?

Section 2

1.	E	6.	D	11.	C	16.	B	21.	A
2.	C	7.	D	12.	B	17.	D	22.	C
3.	B	8.	A	13.	E	18.	E	23.	B
4.	C	9.	E	14.	A	19.	D	24.	B
5.	A	10.	B	15.	C	20.	A	25.	C

1. Answer: **E**

   Distribute first the negative sign, then combine like terms: $37x - 24x + 15y + 29y = 13x + 44y$. The answer is E.

2. **Answer: C**

    The elements of the set K∩L (intersection of K and L) are those exactly in both sets. Set K indicates that all elements can be divided by 5. To check which elements in set L can be divided by 5, look at the last digit. It should either be 5 or 0. Only 295, 725, and 560 fits the criteria. There are only three elements that are divisible by 5, hence the answer is C

3. **Answer: B**

    To get the slope of the line, use the formula $m = \dfrac{y_2 - y_1}{x_2 - x_1} = \dfrac{5-1}{-2-(-7)} = -\dfrac{4}{5}$. The slope of the line is $-\dfrac{4}{5}$, hence the answer is B.

4. **Answer: C**

    We need to get the perimeter of the fence first. $P = 2l + 2w = 2(16) + 2(12) = 32 + 24 = 56$ yards. After getting the perimeter, multiply the result to the cost for every yard: $56 \times 11.75 = \$658$. The fence costs $\$658$, hence the answer is C.

5. **Answer: A**

    A rectangle has two diagonals with the same length. We can find the length of line AD using the distance formula: $D = \sqrt{(x_1 - x_2)^2 + (y_1 - y_2)^2} = \sqrt{(5-8)^2 + (2-0)^2} = \sqrt{(-3)^2 + (2)^2} = \sqrt{9+4} = \sqrt{13} \approx 3.6$. The length of the diagonal is 3.6 units, hence the answer is A.

6. **Answer: D**

    Let's add the students who scored 70 or less: $54 + 12 = 66$. Then, let's add all the students from the ranges: $18 + 49 + 67 + 54 + 12 = 200$. To get what percent of the students scored 70 or less, divide the sum of the students who scored 70 or less with the sum of all the students: $\dfrac{66}{200} = 0.33$ or 33%. 33% of the students who took the test scored 70 or less, hence the answer is D.

7. **Answer: D**

    To get area of a parallelogram, use the formula $A = b \times h = 8 \times 10 = 80$ cm². The area of the parallelogram is 80 cm², hence the answer is D.

8. **Answer: A**

    Since the expression has the same denominator, we only need to evaluate the numerator: $\dfrac{11}{15} + \dfrac{7}{15} - \dfrac{12}{15} = \dfrac{11 + 7 - 12}{15} = \dfrac{6}{15} = \dfrac{2}{5}$. The answer is A.

9. **Answer: E**

    Let x be the percentage. Let's set up a proportion: $\dfrac{x}{100} = \dfrac{88}{400}$. Cross-multiply to get the value of x: $400x = 8800 \Rightarrow x = 22\%$. 88 is 22% of 400, hence the answer is E.

10. Answer: B

Multiply the amount Kayla received for each hour that Chris works with 14.5 hours to get the total amount she will receive: 2.00 × 14.5 = $29.00. Kayla will receive $29.00, hence the answer is B.

11. Answer: C

Let x be the number. $\sqrt{x} = 43$, raise both sides to the power of 2 to get x. $x = (43)^2 = 1849$. The number is 1849, hence the answer is C.

12. Answer: B

A number is divisible by 9 without a remainder when each of its digits add up to a number that can be divided by 9. For option A, 5 + 3 + 9 = 17 ÷ 9 = 1 r 8. For option B, 5 + 4 + 0 = 9 ÷ 9 = 1. For option C, 5 + 3 + 7 = 15 ÷ 9 = 1 r 6. For option D, 5 + 3 + 3 = 11 ÷ 9 = 1 r 2. For option E, 5 + 4 + 2 = 11 ÷ 9 = 1 r 2. Among the choices, only option B is divisible by 9 (no remainder), hence the answer is B.

13. Answer: E

If Neil will walk 6 km more with the same speed, then it will take another 30 minutes. If we will add the total time he walked, then we will get 45 minutes (first 15 minutes + the additional 30 minutes). 45 minutes is $\frac{3}{4}$ of an hour, hence the answer is E.

14. Answer: A

A dozen, by definition, is a set of 12. Half of a dozen will be a set of 6, so Liam has 6 eggs. Multiply 6 and $\frac{1}{3}$ to get the number of eggs he cooked. $6 \times \frac{1}{3} = 2$. Liam cooked two eggs, hence the answer is A.

15. Answer: C

If the perimeter of ABC is 4 times the perimeter of XYZ, and the perimeter of ABC is 36 m, then the perimeter of XYZ is $\frac{1}{4}$ of 36 m, which is 9 m. Now that we have the perimeter of XYZ, divide the perimeter by 3 to get the length of each side. 9 ÷ 3 = 3 m. Each side of the equilateral triangle XYZ measures 3 m, hence the answer is C.

16. Answer: B

There are 20 dice. Since there are 4 blue dice, the remaining 16 are non-blue dice. To get the probability of getting a non-blue dice, divide 16 by 20 and then multiply the quotient with 100 to get the percentage. 16 ÷ 20 = 0.8 × 100 = 80%. The probability of getting a dice that is not blue is 80%, hence the answer is B.

17. Answer: D

To get the perimeter of a trapezoid, use the formula $P = b_1 + b_2 + s_1 + s_2 = 4 + 6 + 5 + 6 = 21$ units. The perimeter of the trapezoid is 21 u, hence the answer is D.

18. **Answer: E**

Let $4x$ be the number of doctors and $7x$ the number of nurses. $4x + 7x = 121 \Rightarrow 11x = 121 \Rightarrow x = 11$. $4x = 4(11) = 44$, $7x = 7(11) = 77$. There are 44 doctors and 77 nurses. Subtract to get the difference: $77 - 44 = 33$. There are 33 more nurses than doctors, hence the answer is E.

19. **Answer: D**

The set is composed of consecutive squares. $1^2, 2^2, 3^2, 4^2, 5^2, 6^2, 7^2 \Rightarrow 1, 4, 9, 16, 25, 36, 49$. To get the value of a, get the square of 8: $8^2 = 64$. The value of a is 64, hence the answer is D.

20. **Answer: A**

Mode is the most repeated value in the given set of data. Rearrange the set to ascending order: 127, 127, 458, 458, 458, 458, 567, 678, 967, 967. The most repeated value is 458 with 4 counts, hence the answer is A.

21. **Answer: A**

Median is the middle value of the given set of data. Rearrange the set to ascending order: 12, 18, 24, 29, 30, 33, 56, 64, 74. The middle value is 30, which is the 5th value, hence the answer is A.

22. **Answer: C**

Distribute the "negative sign" to the subtrahend, and then combine like terms. $4x - 5x + 2 - 3x - 1 \Rightarrow 4x - 5x - 3x + 2 - 1 = -4x + 1$. The answer is C.

23. **Answer: B**

Substitute the value of x, y, and z. $xyz = 5 \times 3 \times 8 = 120$. The product of xyz is 120, hence the answer is B.

24. **Answer: B**

To get the area of a triangle, we can use the formula $A = \dfrac{1}{2}bh$. We can substitute b with y and h with x. $450 = \dfrac{1}{2}(20)y \Rightarrow 450 = 10y \Rightarrow y = 45$. The value of y is 45 in, hence the answer is B.

25. **Answer: C**

Clint brought 40 cookies (4 boxes of cookies × 10 cookies each box). He was left with 4 cookies, so the rest (36 cookies) were consumed by him and his friends. He ate 6 cookies, so the remaining 30 cookies were given to his friends. He gave 3 cookies to each friend, so let's divide 30 by 3: $30 \div 3 = 10$. Clint gave the cookies to his 10 friends, hence the answer is C.

Section 3

1. A	7. B	13. C	19. D	25. A	31. B	37. C
2. B	8. C	14. A	20. D	26. B	32. C	38. A
3. C	9. D	15. B	21. A	27. C	33. D	39. B
4. D	10. A	16. B	22. C	28. D	34. A	40. B
5. D	11. C	17. A	23. B	29. D	35. C	
6. C	12. D	18. D	24. A	30. C	36. B	

1. The correct answer is A. The story is set in Egypt. The first sentence tells us that due to scarce rain, water is precious in Egypt.

2. The correct answer is B. When there are no clouds in the sky to block the rays of the sun, we can imply that the weather is extremely hot.

3. The correct answer is C. They would not know what to think of us, if we should ask for milk, for they never heard of it being used in coffee.

4. The correct answer is D. The coffee is very fragrant, for the berry is crushed, instead of being ground.

5. The correct answer is D. Muddy was used to describe the coffee in the story. It means cloudy with sediment.

6. The correct answer is C. The word "ground" as used in the story refers to the past tense of grind, which is the action of reducing to fine particles, as by pounding or crushing; bray, triturate, or pulverize.

7. The correct answer is B. The article is about Maya's campaign on raising awareness about plastic produce stickers.

8. The correct answer is C. Maya's campaign has two goals: to raise awareness about and to push plastic stickers to be banned.

9. The correct answer is D. One of the main issues with most plastic stickers is that they don't break down in the compost, which can contaminate the soil if used in your backyard and can end up in waterways such as rivers and lakes.

10. The correct answer is A. According to Jane Proctor, vice president of the Canadian Produce Marketing Association (CPMA), plastic is currently the most durable material. Stickers have to be able to stay on the items while traveling to the store and on the shelves.

11. The correct answer is C. According to Jane Proctor, vice president of the Canadian Produce Marketing Association (CPMA), plastic is currently the most durable material. Stickers have to be able to stay on the items while traveling to the store and on the shelves.

12. The correct answer is D. Plastic PLU stickers are used by the produce industry to label bulk fruits and vegetables that are sold loose at the grocery store. They are used to make sure customers are paying the right price for an item and to prevent items from getting mixed up.

13. The correct answer is C. The current issue with banning PLU is durability. There are substitutes that can be made of paper and other compostable materials but may not be able to stay on the items while traveling to the store and on the shelves. We may assume that if this issue can be addressed, banning PLU under the single-use plastic ban will be considered.

14. The correct answer is A. The pastor was kind enough to offer his home to the stranger he just saw as he presumed, he's a stranger to the place.

15. The correct answer is B. When the pastor offered his cottage as accommodation to the stranger, he said it was growing dark, which meant the sun was about to set and it would be nighttime soon.

16. The correct answer is B. The pastor thought the stranger's singing came from the heart, which meant that it was sincere.

17. The correct answer is A. "Look up" is a phrasal verb that means to search for and find a piece of information in a book or database. However, in the story, it means to see her as a role model. In this case, they were both looking up to God.

18. The correct answer is D. To suppose means to assume (something), as for the sake of argument or as part of a proposition or theory.

19. The correct answer is D. The article was an interview with Tara Ivanochko, an environmental scientist and University of British Columbia professor about the new research on the ozone, which may nearly be in the clear, the concern with the ozone, and what was done to help our ozone.

20. The correct answer is D. The international agreement agreed upon to remove certain chemicals from production like refrigerants (a chemical used to make things cool) that would get released into the atmosphere and break down the ozone.

21. The correct answer is A. That agreement was called the Montreal Protocol, held here in Canada in 1987.

22. The correct answer is C. The ozone is a see-through layer that surrounds the Earth and keeps the sun's strong, harmful rays from burning us.

23. The correct answer is B. With the way the atmosphere circulates, many chemicals will concentrate in the polar areas of Earth, so ozone holes will start to develop in those areas.

24. The correct answer is A. The story was describing the area surrounding Adalbert's parents which was abundant with farm animals. Blissful means full of, abounding in, enjoying, or conferring bliss; not troubled by any hint of unease or discontent.

25. The correct answer is A. The descriptions best depict that the setting is by the countryside which is a land and scenery of a rural area.

26. The correct answer is B. The short story started with descriptions of what surrounds the large and beautiful farm belonging to Adalbert's parents.

27. The correct answer is C. "To cease" means to stop, discontinue, or to come to an end.

28. The correct answer is D. The word "fear" was used in the phrase "which caused fear". In this phrase, it was used as a noun, which means a distressing emotion aroused by impending danger, evil, or pain. It can also be used as a verb.

29. The correct answer is D. Mother Barru was described as the queen of the community and was a woman of good sense. However, her good humor ceased only on two occasions—when a boy on the farm got drunk and when a hen hid her eggs at a distance.

30. The correct answer is C. The article is about the proposed resolution on climate justice by Vanuatu. Although not legally binding, this could propel the climate justice movement forward and serve as a huge victory for smaller nations.

31. The correct answer is B. The article gives information about the recent proposal by a tiny Pacific island nation on a resolution on climate justice at the United Nations General Assembly Meeting, which could propel the climate justice movement forward and serve as a huge victory for smaller nations.

32. The correct answer is C. The new resolution calls upon the International Court of Justice (ICJ) to issue an advisory opinion on nations that don't meet their climate obligations, which passed with the support of a core group of 17 nations and 132 co-sponsoring nations.

33. The correct answer is D. Vanuatu is a tiny Pacific island nation with a population of just 320,000.

34. The correct answer is A. The word "advisory" was used in the phrase "to issue an advisory opinion." Advisory means having the power or duty to advise. It can also be used as a noun.

35. The correct answer is C. "To propel" means to impel or urge onward.

36. The correct answer is B. Their goal was to spark an emotional reaction with the lack of action by governments to stop burning fossil fuels and address the climate crisis.

37. The correct answer is C. It would save 5.4 million tons of carbon dioxide per year.

38. The correct answer is A. The article explained why many activists attack famous paintings. It gives us a better understanding that their goal is to see people extend the protectiveness they feel toward a famous painting to life on Earth.

39. The correct answer is B. "Backlash" means a strong or violent reaction, as to some social or political change. Synonyms are reaction and resistance.

40. The correct answer is B. "Toward" is a preposition that means in the direction or vicinity of, or, with regard to. In the phrase "feel toward a famous painting," toward was used as with regard to a famous painting.

Section 4

1. D	11. A	21. C	31. B	41. B	51. A
2. A	12. B	22. A	32. C	42. A	52. B
3. B	13. C	23. A	33. D	43. C	53. C
4. C	14. D	24. B	34. A	44. B	54. D
5. C	15. D	25. D	35. B	45. A	55. B
6. A	16. B	26. C	36. D	46. B	56. C
7. D	17. A	27. C	37. B	47. D	57. A
8. A	18. B	28. A	38. C	48. A	58. B
9. B	19. C	29. A	39. D	49. C	59. A
10. C	20. D	30. B	40. A	50. A	60. B

1. The correct answer is D. "Sudden" means happening, coming, made, or done quickly, without warning, or unexpectedly. Synonyms are unexpected and hasty.

2. The correct answer is A. "To adjust" means to change (something) so that it fits, corresponds, or conforms; adapt; accommodate. Synonyms are to modify and alter.

3. The correct answer is B. "Worried" is having or characterized by worry; concerned; anxious. Synonyms are bothered and concerned.

4. The correct answer is C. "Productive" means producing readily or abundantly; fertile. Synonyms are fruitful and profitable.

5. The correct answer is C. "To boast" means to speak with exaggeration and excessive pride, especially about oneself. Synonyms are to brag or gloat.

6. The correct answer is A. "Unpredictable" means not predictable; not to be foreseen or foretold. Synonyms are erratic, uncertain, and unstable.

7. The correct answer is D. "Brief" means lasting or taking a short time; of short duration. Synonyms are quick and swift.

8. The correct answer is A. "Doubtful" means of uncertain outcome or result. Synonyms are unsure and uncertain.

9. The correct answer is B. "Economical" means avoiding waste or extravagance; thrifty. Synonyms are practical and cost-effective.

10. The correct answer is C. "To attempt" means to make an effort at; try; undertake; seek.

11. The correct answer is A. "To hesitate" means to be reluctant or wait to act because of fear, indecision, or disinclination. Synonyms are to pause and ponder.

12. The correct answer is B. "To thrive" means to grow or develop vigorously; to flourish. Synonyms are to develop and grow.

13. The correct answer is C. "Pleasing" means giving pleasure; agreeable; gratifying. Synonyms are charming and delightful.

14. The correct answer is D. "Random" means proceeding, made, or occurring without definite aim, reason, or pattern. Synonyms are incidental and irregular.

15. The correct answer is D. "To overwhelm" means to overcome completely in mind or feeling. Synonyms are to overcome and overpower.

16. The correct answer is B. "Noble" means distinguished by rank or title. Synonyms are dignified and great.

17. The correct answer is A. "To attract" means to draw by appealing to the emotions or senses, by stimulating interest, or by exciting admiration; allure; invite. Synonyms are to entice and captivate.

18. The correct answer is B. "To imitate" means to follow or endeavor to follow as a model or example. Synonyms are to mimic and replicate.

19. The correct answer is C. "Definite" means clearly defined or determined; not vague or general; fixed; precise; exact.

20. The correct answer is D. "Famous" means having a widespread reputation, usually of a favorable nature; renowned; celebrated.

21. The correct answer is C. "Difficult" means not easily or readily done; requiring much labor, skill, or planning to be performed successfully; hard.

22. The correct answer is A. "To honor" means to hold in honor or high respect, revere. Synonyms are to commemorate and appreciate.

23. The correct answer is A. "Faithful" means steady in allegiance or affection; loyal; constant. Synonyms are devoted and loyal.

24. The correct answer is B. "Obvious" means easily seen, recognized, or understood; open to view or knowledge; evident.

25. The correct answer is D. "Immediately" means without lapse of time; without delay; instantly; at once.

26. The correct answer is C. "To desire" means to wish or long for; crave; want.

27. The correct answer is C. "To cease" means to stop; discontinue.

28. The correct answer is A. Disgust, as a noun, means a strong distaste; nausea; loathing.

29. The correct answer is A. A breach is a gap made in a wall, fortification, line of soldiers, etc.; rift; fissure.

30. The correct answer is B. "Suitable" means such as to suit; appropriate; fitting; becoming.

31. The correct answer is B. The first pair has season–clothing relationship. You wear a sweater in winter; you wear a hat in summer.

32. The correct answer is C. The first pair has container–food/beverage relationship. You drink tea from a teacup; you eat ice cream from a cone.

33. The correct answer is D. The first pair has item–body part relationship. You use a comb for your hair; you wear slippers for your feet.

34. The correct answer is A. The first pair has weather/temperature–reaction relationship. When it's too hot, you sweat; when it's too cold, you shiver.

35. The correct answer is B. The first pair has animal–habitat relationship. Birds dwell in the sky; fishes live in the sea.

36. The correct answer is D. The first pair has celestial body–time of day relationship. The sun rises in the morning; the moon shines at night.

37. The correct answer is B. The first pair is antonyms. Dark is the opposite of light; hot is the opposite of cold.

38. The correct answer is C. The first pair is antonyms. Open is the opposite of close; free is the opposite of captive.

39. The correct answer is D. The first pair is antonyms. Happy is the opposite of sad; beautiful is the opposite of ugly.

40. The correct answer is A. The first pair is antonyms. Clever is the opposite of dumb; wise is the opposite of ignorant.

41. The correct answer is B. The first pair has male–female title relationship. Queen is the female counterpart of a king; duchess is the female counterpart of a duke.

42. The correct answer is A. The first pair has profession–workplace relationship. A doctor works at a hospital; a chef works in a restaurant.

43. The correct answer is C. The first pair has item–action relationship. A pen is used to write something; a camera is used to capture photos or video.

44. The correct answer is B. The first pair has item–action relationship. You sit on a chair; you sleep in a bed.

45. The correct answer is A. The first pair has animal–common food relationship. A squirrel is commonly known to eat an acorn; a rabbit is commonly known to eat carrots.

46. The correct answer is B. A teacher teaches her students; a parent care for his/her children.

47. The correct answer is D. The first pair has item–purpose relationship. A clock is used to tell time; a thermometer is used to measure temperature.

48. The correct answer is A. The first pair has transportation–action relationship. A plane flies; a ship sails.

49. The correct answer is C. The first pair has object–action relationship. You count numbers; you read words.

50. The correct answer is A. The first pair has group name–members relationship. A crew consists of a group of sailors; a company consists of a group of solders.

51. The correct answer is A. The first pair has object–action relationship. You climb a ladder; you sew with a needle.

52. The correct answer is B. The first pair has action–feeling relationship. You laugh when you're happy; you cry when you're sad.

53. The correct answer is C. The first pair is antonyms. Quiet is the opposite of noisy; silent is the opposite of loud.

54. The correct answer is D. The first pair has source–product relationship. You can make jam with strawberries; you can make cheese with milk.

55. The correct answer is B. The first pair has event–act relationship. There is mourning when there is death; there is a celebration when there is new life.

56. The correct answer is C. The first pair has color–category relationship. red is a primary color; green is a secondary color.

57. The correct answer is A. The first pair is synonyms. To admire is to adore; to adapt is to conform. Other synonyms for adapt are to alter, modify, and revise.

58. The correct answer is B. The first pair is synonyms. Agile is synonymous with lively; sluggish is synonymous with inactive. Other synonyms for sluggish are lethargic and slow.

59. The correct answer is A. The first pair is synonyms. Ambiguous is synonymous with unclear; precise is synonymous with definite. Other synonyms for precise are accurate and specific.

60. The correct answer is B. The first pair has item–purpose relationship. You put the earphones in your ears to use them; you type on the keyboard with your fingers.

Section 5

1. A	6. D	11. D	16. C	21. A
2. B	7. C	12. C	17. C	22. B
3. E	8. A	13. B	18. E	23. A
4. B	9. E	14. B	19. D	24. C
5. C	10. E	15. A	20. C	25. B

1. Answer: **A**

   Find the greatest common factor (GCF) of the ratio. The GCF will be 30. Let's divide each number by 30 to the simplest form of the ratio $\frac{210}{90} \div 30 = \frac{7}{3}$ or 7:3. Answer is A.

2. **Answer: B**

Let's use cross-multiplication to get the value of x: $7x = 4(x + 3) \Rightarrow 7x = 4x + 12 \Rightarrow 3x = 12 \Rightarrow x = 4$. The value of x is 4, hence the answer is B.

3. **Answer: E**

Let x be the number $0.30x = 324 \Rightarrow x = 1080$. 324 is the 30% of 1080, hence the answer is E.

4. **Answer: B**

Find the common denominator of the equation. The Least Common Multiple (LCM) of 15 and 5 is 15. $\dfrac{11}{15} - \dfrac{3}{5} = \dfrac{11-9}{15} = \dfrac{2}{15}$. Answer is B.

5. **Answer: C**

To get the perimeter of a triangle, use the formula $P = s + s + s = 8 + 9 + 10 = 27$ cm. The perimeter of the triangle is 27 cm, hence the answer is C.

6. **Answer: D**

To get the perimeter of a square, use the formula $P = 4s = 4 (5) = 20$ in. The perimeter is 20 in, hence the answer is D.

7. **Answer: C**

To get the area of a parallelogram, use the formula $A = b \times h = 8 \times 9 = 72$ in². The area of the parallelogram is 72 in², hence the answer is C.

8. **Answer: A**

To get the length of the line segment, use the distance formula $D = \sqrt{(x_1 - x_2)^2 + (y_1 - y_2)^2}$ $= \sqrt{(-2-3)^2 + (4-2)^2} = \sqrt{(-5)^2 + (2)^2} = \sqrt{25+4} = \sqrt{29} = 5.39$ units. The length of the line segment is approximately 5.39 units, hence the answer is A.

9. **Answer: E**

By definition, a point with a negative x-coordinate and a negative y-coordinate lies in Quadrant III on the coordinate plane, hence the answer is E.

10. **Answer: E**

To get the slope of the line, use the formula $m = \dfrac{y_2 - y_1}{x_2 - x_1} = \dfrac{3-5}{2-4} = \dfrac{-2}{-2} = 1$. The slope of the line is 1, hence the answer is E.

11. **Answer: D**

   Let's get the total TV viewing for Carla and Luis for each day of the week. Sunday: 4.2 + 3.9 = 8.1, Monday: 1.2 + 1.5 = 2.7, Tuesday: 1.6 + 1.4 = 3, Wednesday: 1.3 + 1.3 = 2.6, Thursday: 1.5 + 1.5 = 3, Friday: 1.1 + 1.3 = 2.4, Saturday: 3.6 + 3.5 = 7.1. Among the days of the week, Sunday has the highest number of hours for TV viewing, hence the answer is D.

12. **Answer: C**

   Let's get the total TV viewing for Carla and Luis for each day of the week. Sunday: 4.2 + 3.9 = 8.1, Monday: 1.2 + 1.5 = 2.7, Tuesday: 1.6 + 1.4 = 3, Wednesday: 1.3 + 1.3 = 2.6, Thursday: 1.5 + 1.5 = 3, Friday: 1.1 + 1.3 = 2.4, Saturday: 3.6 + 3.5 = 7.1. Among the days of the week, Friday has the lowest number of hours for TV viewing, hence the answer is C.

13. **Answer: B**

   Median is the middle value of the given set of data. Rearrange the set to ascending order: 90, 91, 92, 94, 95. The middle value is 92, which is the 3rd value, hence the answer is B.

14. **Answer: B**

   Mean is the average value of the given set of data. Add all the data, then divide it with the total number of data to get the average. $\dfrac{421 + 563 + 398 + 236 + 107}{5} = \dfrac{1725}{5} = 345$. The mean is 345, hence the answer is B.

15. **Answer: A**

   Find the product: $6b \times 12b = 72b^2$. The answer is A.

16. **Answer: C**

   Let x be the number. $\dfrac{1}{4}x + 20 = 56 \implies \dfrac{1}{4}x = 36 \implies x = 144$. The number is 144, hence the answer is C.

17. **Answer: C**

   The subset should be composed of prime number—can only be multiplied by 1 and the number itself. For option A, it contains 21, which has 4 factors. For option B, it contains 9 which has 4 factors and 12 which has 6 factors. For option D, it contains 15, which has 4 factors. For option E, it contains 27 which has 4 factors and 30 which has 8 factors. Only option C contains values that are all prime numbers, hence the answer is C.

18. **Answer: E**

   To get the slope of the line, use the formula $m = \dfrac{y_2 - y_1}{x_2 - x_1} = \dfrac{-6 - (-4)}{-3 - 5} = \dfrac{-2}{-8} = \dfrac{1}{4}$. The slope of the line is $\dfrac{1}{4}$, hence the answer is E.

19. **Answer: D**

   To get the length of the side of a square, use the formula $s = \sqrt{A} \Rightarrow s = \sqrt{121} = 11$. The length of the side is 11 units. To get the perimeter, use the formula $P = 4s = 4(11) = 44$ units. The perimeter of the square is 44 units, hence the answer is D.

20. **Answer: C**

   To divide a fraction with a fraction, get the reciprocal of the divisor and change the operation to multiplication: $\frac{4}{5} \div \frac{5}{6} = \frac{4}{5} \times \frac{6}{5} = \frac{24}{25}$. The answer is C.

21. **Answer: A**

   To get the percentage of the students who attended the field trip, divide the number of present by the total number of students: $27 \div 30 = 0.9 \times 100 = 90\%$. 90% of the class went to the field trip, hence the answer is A.

22. **Answer: B**

   To get the perimeter of an equilateral triangle, use the formula $P = 3s = 3(4) = 12$ in. The perimeter of the triangle is 12 in, hence the answer is B.

23. **Answer: A**

   To get the perimeter of a rectangle, use the formula $P = 2l + 2w$. Substitute: $72 = 2(6x) + 2(3x) \Rightarrow 72 = 12x + 6x \Rightarrow 72 = 18x \Rightarrow x = 4$. The value of x is 4, hence the answer is A.

24. **Answer: C**

   The point $(0,7)$ does not move in any direction on the x-axis, but does move 7 units upward on the y-axis, hence this point is located on the y-axis. The answer is C.

25. **Answer: B**

   Range is the difference between the maximum and minimum values of a dataset. Rearrange the dataset in ascending order: 34, 42, 48, 50, 67, 81, 95. With the given dataset, the minimum value is 34 and the maximum value is 95. Subtract: $95 - 34 = 61$. The range is 61, hence the answer is B.

SSAT Middle Level Exam 3

WRITING SAMPLE

Time—25 minutes

Directions:

Read the following topics carefully. Take a few minutes to select the topic you find more interesting. Think about the topic and organize your thoughts on a scrap paper before you begin writing.

Topic A: If I were given a superpower, I...

Topic B: If I had to go back to a ...

Circle your selection: Topic A or Topic B. Write your essay for the selected topic on the paper provided. Your essay should NOT exceed two pages and must be written in pencil. Be sure that your handwriting is legible and that you must stay within the lines and margins.

_____
_____
_____
_____
_____
_____
_____
_____
_____
_____
_____
_____
_____
_____

SECTION 2

QUANTITATIVE MATH

Time—30 minutes

25 Questions

In this section, there are five possible answers after each problem. Choose which one is best.

Example

5,413 – 4,827 =

(A) 586
(B) 596
(C) 696
(D) 1,586
(E) 1,686

Answer

● Ⓑ Ⓒ Ⓓ Ⓔ

The correct answer to this question is lettered A, so space A is marked.

---

1. Solve for x: $4(x + 15) = 120$

   (A) 60   (B) 35   (C) 15   (D) 30   (E) 17

2. Line AE is a straight line. It measures 64 cm. Assuming that AB, BC, CD, and DE are line segments of AE, if AB = x, BC = $x + 2$, CD = $3x + 6$, DE = $x - 10$, how long is AB?

   (A) 11   (B) 12   (C) 10   (D) 39   (E) 13

3. A square is 9 ft long on each side. How many smaller squares, each 3 ft on a side can be cut out of the larger square?

   (A) 18   (B) 9   (C) 3   (D) 6   (E) 5

4. A square has perimeter 170.8 cm. What is the length of one side?

   (A) 40.7 cm   (B) 42.2 cm   (C) 47.7 cm   (D) 47.2 cm   (E) 42.7 cm

5. Express the quotient as a fraction in lowest term: $3\frac{4}{7} \div 2\frac{6}{7}$

   (A) $1\frac{1}{2}$ (B) $1\frac{1}{4}$ (C) $\frac{3}{4}$ (D) $1\frac{3}{4}$ (E) $\frac{7}{4}$

6. Express $\dfrac{19}{500}$ as a decimal.

   (A) 0.38   (B) 0.83   (C) 0.083   (D) 0.038   (E) 3.8

7. Lyra, Lina, and Leo add up all of their ages and get a total of 33. If they do the same thing two years from now, what will be the total?

   (A) 40   (B) 37   (C) 39   (D) 35   (E) cannot be determined

8. What is the difference between 37 and the product of 6 and 4?

   (A) 17   (B) 12   (C) 13   (D) 15   (E) 19

9. Solve for x: $x - 37 = 73$

   (A) 63   (B) 36   (C) 100   (D) 101   (E) 110

10. Sarah borrowed 54 books in the last six months. She returned half of them and then borrowed 7 more. How many books does she have now?

    (A) 34 books   (B) 37 books   (C) 35 books   (D) 30 books   (E) 36 books

11. Suppose you know the values of variables in the expression $a + b \times c - d$ and you want to evaluate the expression; in which order will you carry out the operation?

    (A) multiplying, subtracting, adding

    (B) adding, multiplying, subtracting

    (C) subtracting, adding, multiplying

    (D) multiplying, adding, subtracting

    (E) adding, subtracting, multiplying

12. Leonard bought a pencil using a \$10 bill and received b dollars in change. Which of the following describes how much Leonard paid for the pencil?

    (A) $10 + b$ (B) $10 - b$ (C) $b + 10$ (D) $b - 10$ (E) cannot be determined

13. Solve for z: $\dfrac{30}{75} = \dfrac{z}{15}$

    (A) 7.5   (B) 5   (C) 6.5   (D) 5.5   (E) 6

For questions 14 and 15, please refer to the figure below.

14. Given that $a = 15$ cm, $b = 20$ cm, and $h = 9$ cm, what is the area of the parallelogram?

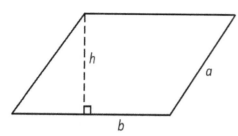

(A) 160 cm²   (B) 140 cm²   (C) 120 cm²   (D) 180 cm²   (E) 150 cm²

15. Given that a and the line opposite to it is parallel; b and the line opposite to it is parallel, what would be the perimeter of the parallelogram if $a = 19$ in and $b = 23$ in?

(A) 86 in   (B) 84 in   (C) 80 in   (D) 88 in   (E) 82 in

16. Supposed that the figure below is a cube, if each side measures 8 cm, what would be the volume?

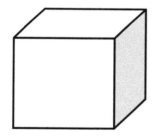

(A) 512 cm³   (B) 64 cm³   (C) 521 cm³   (D) 46 cm³   (E) 32 cm³

17. Lolita bought a $\frac{1}{8}$ of a pound of sugar for $3.00. What will be the price per pound?

(A) $24.00   (B) $16.00   (C) $14.00   (D) $8.00   (E) $10.00

18. 126 is 120% of what number?

(A) 105   (B) 102   (C) 110   (D) 150   (E) 120

19. Rectangle KLMN has an area of 120 cm². If the width of the rectangle is 10 cm, what is the perimeter?

(A) 48 cm   (B) 38 cm   (C) 44 cm   (D) 42 cm   (E) 40 cm

20. The width of a rectangle is half of its length. If the width is given as w, what is the perimeter of the rectangle in terms of w?

(A) 10w (B) 2w (C) 8w (D) 4w (E) 6w

21. Write 75% as a fraction in simplest form.

    (A) $\frac{6}{8}$ (B) $\frac{25}{100}$ (C) $\frac{3}{4}$ (D) $\frac{1}{4}$ (E) $\frac{75}{100}$

22. Evaluate $\frac{3}{5} \div \frac{9}{10}$

    (A) $\frac{3}{5}$ (B) $\frac{2}{3}$ (C) $\frac{1}{3}$ (D) $\frac{2}{5}$ (E) $\frac{1}{5}$

23. Which of the following expressions is equivalent to the expression $-3(-2x + 9)$?

    (A) $6x + 27$ (B) $6x - 27$ (C) $-6x - 27$ (D) $-6x + 27$ (E) $-6x - 9$

24. Which of the following is an example of an application of the distributive property?

    (A) $2 \times (3 \times 4) = (2 \times 3) \times 4$

    (B) $9 + (1 + 7) = (9 + 1) + 7$

    (C) $3 \times (8 + 11) = 3 \times 8 + 3 \times 11$

    (D) $3 + (8 \times 11) = (8 \times 11) + 3$

    (E) $1 \times (3 \times 4) = 3 \times 4$

25. Evaluate: $212 - 157.67$

    (A) 54.43 (B) 53.43 (C) 53.33 (D) 54.44 (E) 54.33

READING COMPREHENSION

Time—40 minutes
40 Questions

Read each passage carefully and then answer the questions about it. For each question, decide on the basis of the passage which one of the choices best answers the question.

"Well, I did not see you yesterday, looking for a place in Water Street?" "I was down there, sir, looking for a place." "Why did you not take that place which the gentleman had for you in the large shop?" "Because, sir, they kept open shop on Sabbath, and mother would not wish me to work on the Lord's day."

"You did not keep the piece of gold that you found on the floor, as you were coming into the street; why didn't you?" "Because it was not mine, sir; and I thought that the gentleman of the shop would find the owner sooner than I should."

"He did, my boy, it was my money. Did you not get a place yesterday?" "No, sir; all the places were full, and nobody knew me." "Well, my boy, you may go now, and tell your mother that you have a place. Come to me very early in the morning- your teacher will tell you where I live."

John went home with his heart and his eyes so full, that he could hardly see the street, or anything as he went along.

From A teacher's gift *by Brown, Taggard & Chase*

1. After reading the passage, we can assume that Sabbath is

   (A) a rest day   (B) a national holiday   (C) someone's birthday   (D) a workday

2. Based on the sir's response to John not taking the money he found on the floor, we may assume that he felt

   (A) angry   (B) grateful   (C) suspicious   (D) disappointed

3. What character does the passage imply John has?

   (A) treacherous   (B) opportunist   (C) kind-hearted   (D) lazy

4. What feeling does the phrase "his heart and his eyes so full" imply?

   (A) loneliness   (B) anger   (C) melancholy   (D) happiness

5. Which is the simple form of the verb "were"?

    (A) where   (B) wear   (C) is   (D) are

6. Why didn't John take the offer to work at the large shop?

    (A) they only wanted a part-timer

    (B) they kept open shop on Sabbath

    (C) they offer low wages

    (D) they are full

Soon there is a change upon the scene—the signals of distress are silent—shrieks are heard no longer. Oh! can it be that perhaps hundreds have perished in that moment of time—that many a brave, loving heart has ceased to beat forever?

It would indeed seem to be the case, for not another sound is heard, and the silence is even more terrible than the past tumult.

Morning dawns, and as the first ray of light shines in the eastern heaven, many are on the beach to learn if any from the wreck have been washed ashore, and to glean tidings of their own comrades. As yet nothing had been found. The coast guardsmen on duty, pacing up and down, suddenly stops his walk: he is attracted by a strange sound near him. He listens: the sound is repeated, but he cannot tell what is resembles. It is certainly not like a human cry. He looks around the edge of a rock, from whence it seems to come, and now it is more audible; it is like the feeble moaning of a dog in pain.

From Birdie and her dog *by E. C. (Edith Caroline) Phillips (Author)*

7. What does the word "distress" mean?

    (A) relief in affliction

    (B) freedom from labor, pain, or physical annoyance

    (C) great pain, anxiety, or sorrow; suffering

    (D) free from commotion or tumult

8. What does the phrase "heart has ceased to beat forever" imply?

    (A) death   (B) heartbreak   (C) immortality   (D) none of the above

9. What part of speech is the word "dawns" as used in the passage?

    (A) verb   (B) noun   (C) adjective   (D) adverb

10. Which is synonymous to the word "glean"?

    (A) disperse   (B) gather   (C) divide   (D) refuse

11. What does "audible" mean?

(A) to work at anything in an irregular or superficial manner

(B) copy added to a completed story

(C) fit to be eaten as food

(D) capable of being heard

12. After reading the passage, we can imply that the setting is after a?

(A) ceremony   (B) celebration   (C) violent commotion at sea   (D) planned gathering

13. What does the word "feeble" mean?

(A) lacking in volume, loudness

(B) capable, effective

(C) effective, powerful, forceful

(D) healthy, strong

"How it has risen since morning!" said Rose. "That post was out of the water then, and now it must be at least a foot beneath it."

"And how fast it runs!" said Clara. "Let's drop sticks in and see them sail."

So, the children played for some time. Then Charlie, looking up the stream, called out,

"Why, there is a kitten coming down! I can hear her meow."

Quick as a flash Dick ran off the bridge and down the edge of the water. He picked up a stick as he ran, and just as he reached the brink pussy came by. He sieved a branch that hung near and reached forward to her. Fortunately, she was swept into a little corner where the current was not strong. She put out one paw and clung to the stick, and Dick drew her gently to shore.

A wet and wretched object she was, as she clambered up the bank, and sank down all drenched and panting.

Rose, Clara, and all the other girls, all ran down to Dick.

From Lost kitten *by McLoughlin Bros.*

14. Where is the setting of the passage?

(A) at the farm   (B) by a stream   (C) a hilltop   (D) a garden

15. What does the word "drenched" mean?

(A) knot up tightly

(B) not stale or spoiled

(C) wet thoroughly; soaked

(D) power of disposal or control

16. What does the phrase "quick as a flash" mean?

(A) not as quick enough   (B) speedy enough to catch up   (C) always one step ahead   (D) very quickly

17. Which is the simple form of the verb "clung"?

(A) clear   (B) clean   (C) clang   (D) cling

18. Which is synonymous to the word "wretched"?

(A) to vomit   (B) unfortunate   (C) dig a hole   (D) craving

The race is on to get more electric cars on the road. President Joe Biden has made electric vehicles (EVs) a priority. By 2030, he'd like half of all new vehicles sold to be zero-emission. It's a response to the climate crisis. Currently, the United States is one of the biggest emitters of greenhouse gases. And more than a quarter of the country's emissions come from gasoline-burning vehicles.

But according to a 2021 survey by Pew Research Center, more than half of U.S. adults don't want gasoline cars to be phased out. They say EVs are expensive and charging them is a hassle. For now, most people plan to stick with gas-powered vehicles. We asked TFK readers what they think about EVs.

Princia Zhou, 9

Chino Hills, California

In my opinion, we should all have electric cars. Our gas cars burn fossil fuels, which are limited resources. These fuels cannot be regenerated. Using them is unsustainable.

But the electricity powering EVs can be generated from renewable energy sources. These include solar and wind power. Think about it: Transportation causes 21% of global carbon-dioxide emissions. That's a huge factor in climate change. Driving EVs could eliminate that. The switch needs to happen soon. Not only to protect the environment, but so we kids can have a brighter and cleaner future.

Kieran Siller, 10

New York, New York

Electric vehicles pollute the planet just as much as, if not more than, gas cars. Think of when you're charging an EV. That power is coming from a power plant, which burns fossil fuels and pollutes the planet. More electric cars just mean more charging. We'd need to build more power plants.

And mining for the elements needed to build EV batteries creates a ton of pollution. If automakers produce all-electric cars, they'll mine for the elements more often. The switch to EVs could destroy the planet. A lot of things are like this. It's not always black-and-white. Both electric and gasoline cars hurt the planet.

From Should All Cars Be Electric? *by Brian S. McGrath*

19. What is the article about?

(A) to discourage people from purchasing electric cars

(B) study behind the greenhouse gases and how to eliminate them

(C) the motion to get more electric cars and discourage the use of gas-powered vehicles; debate of pros and cons

(D) to discourage people from purchasing electric cars

20. What is an EV?

(A) electric vehicles   (B) electric voltage   (C) electric voyage   (D) electronic vial

21. Why does President Joe Biden want electric cars?

(A) as a response to the climate crisis, US being the biggest emitter of greenhouse gases

(B) the country will gain commission for every electric car sold

(C) for business partnership

(D) to stay on trend

22. Why do people from the US not want gasoline cars to be phased out?

(A) need to be imported from another country

(B) EVs are expensive and charging them is a hassle

(C) difficult to obtain license for

(D) take time to learn how to use

23. What is the article's stand on phasing out gasoline-burning vehicles?

(A) agreeing; the article agrees that the switch to EVs will be only beneficial without harmful effects

(B) disagreeing; the article disagrees with EVs since the disadvantages outweigh the advantages

(C) agreeing; the article agrees that the advantages of EVs outweigh the disadvantages

(D) none. Both sides are presented in the article

Sixty-six years ago, there was one human-built object in Earth's orbit: Sputnik, the world's first satellite. It was launched in October 1957. Try to guess how many human-made objects are circling the planet now. Ready?

The answer is 100 trillion. That's the number provided by a team of researchers writing in the journal Science. For years, a mass of junk orbiting Earth has been growing. It's a danger to spacecraft.

The researchers are calling for a global treaty. It would limit the amount of junk in space. Only a "legally binding treaty," they say, can "protect Earth's orbit."

From Collision Course *by Jeffrey Kluger for TIME, adapted by TFK editors*

24. What is the first human-built object launched into the Earth's Orbit?

(A) spacecraft   (B) Apollo   (C) Sputnik   (D) Junk

25. When was the first human-made satellite launched?

(A) October 1975   (B) October 1957   (C) in a tropical island   (D) in a vast desert

26. What is the article about?

   (A) to promote the newest satellite

   (B) feature the 1st satellite to orbit the Earth

   (C) a global treaty was called for the mass of junk orbiting Earth

   (D) to encourage more children to be astronauts in the future

27. What is the objective of the treaty mentioned in the passage?

   (A) to proceed to perform the first or earliest part of some action

   (B) to start again

   (C) to come to an end

   (D) limit the amount of junk in space

28. How many human-made objects are orbiting the planet now?

   (A) 100 trillion   (B) was   (C) beside   (D) fear

29. What does a treaty mean?

   (A) anything that affords particular pleasure or enjoyment

   (B) a formal agreement between two or more states

   (C) characterized by hackneyed expressions, ideas

   (D) none of the above

Sixteen young people are suing the state of Montana. They say its support for fossil fuels is driving climate change. Held v. Montana is not the first youth climate case in the United States. But it's the first to go to trial. The trial is set to begin in June.

The case was filed in 2020. At the time, the kids ranged in age from 2 to 18. Their argument is based on the Montana State Constitution. It says citizens have "the right to a clean and healthful environment." The state is violating its own rule, the youths say.

Montana is one of the country's top producers of coal and oil. In 2011, its lawmakers changed state policy to increase fossil-fuel development. That policy was repealed in March. It's unclear if this will affect the lawsuit.

Lander Busse, 18, is one of the young people in the lawsuit. He told the Helena Independent Record that the youths' mission is to hold Montana's leaders accountable for violating the state constitution. "It's sad that it's falling on us, the youth, to do this," he says, "and not the adults."

From Youth Climate Case *by Cristina Fernandez*

30. What is the main topic of the article?

    (A) about the state's mission to discourage fossil fuel

    (B) where is the greatest source of fossil for fuel

    (C) about Montana's mission to a clean environment

    (D) youth climate case against the state of Montana

31. Which best describes the article?

    (A) emotional   (B) informative   (C) cheerful   (D) melancholic

32. What caused the youth to file a lawsuit against the State?

    (A) to stop the State from discouraging business opportunities for fossil fuel

    (B) promotion of gas-fueled vehicles

    (C) violation on the State's law on the right to a clean and healthy environment for increasing fossil-fuel development

    (D) to mandate recycling day to be every Wednesday of the week

33. How old were the kids involved in the case?

    (A) 21 years old   (B) 17 years old   (C) 16 years older and below 21   (D) age from 2 to 18

34. What does the word "repeal" mean?

    (A) to revoke or withdraw formally

    (B) to ask for aid, support

    (C) the act of asking for something to be given or done

    (D) claim as a right

35. How is the *Held v. Montana* case different from the other youth climate case in the United States?

    (A) first that are taken part of youth

    (B) first youth climate case to go to trial

    (C) fist climate case against a state

    (D) first ever case filed by young ones

In January, an Arizona desert community found itself in a nightmare situation: The water was cut off.

Rio Verde Foothills is made up of about 2,000 homes. For years, many of them relied on water trucked in from the nearby city of Scottsdale. It gets water from the Colorado River. But the river is drying up. Scottsdale says it has to save water for its own residents.

The southwestern United States has experienced drought for more than 20 years. Water supplies are shrinking. Arizona can pump water from underground. But that can't provide half of what's needed. Meanwhile, thousands of new residents arrive every year, and more communities like Rio Verde Foothills are built. There isn't enough groundwater for all those homes.

Some experts say the solution is to import water from outside the state. One idea is to build a desalination plant on Mexico's Sea of Cortez. It would remove salt from the water and pump that water to Arizona through a pipeline. Supporters say this could provide water for decades.

Critics see a different future: environmental destruction. Margaret Wilder is a professor at the University of Arizona, in Tucson. She warns that big projects like this one could be used to justify "much more unsustainable development in the desert in the future."

From Drying Up *by Ciara Nugent adapted by TFK editors*

36. What is the article about?

    (A) sources of water in Arizona

    (B) promotion of a new community

    (C) overpopulation in Arizona

    (D) water shortage in an Arizona desert community and the solutions presented

37. Why was the water for Rio Verde Foothills cut off?

    (A) because of global warming

    (B) the river where they source their water is drying up and can only accommodate their own residents

    (C) because the state will use the river for profit

    (D) there is dam being constructed to hold the water

38. What is the challenge in implementing the solutions to the water shortage?

    (A) shortage in budget   (B) no profit   (C) environmental destruction   (D) the solution will take too much time to realize

39. What is the meaning of "drought"?

    (A) mentally deranged

    (B) produced or shaped by beating with a hammer

    (C) a first or preliminary form of any writing

    (D) an extended shortage

40. Why is pumping underground water not the best solution?

    (A) there isn't enough for all the homes

    (B) there is no tool to dig underground

    (C) it is against the environmental law of the state

    (D) the water is dirty

SECTION 4

VERBAL REASONING

Time—30 minutes
60 Questions

This section consists of two different types of questions. There are directions for each type.

Each of the following questions consists of one word followed by four words or phrases. You have to select a word or phrase whose meaning is closest to the word in capital letters.

Example

SWIFT: (A) clean (B) fancy (C) fast (D) quiet

Answer

(A) (B) ● (D)

1. AFFINITY

    (A) dislike (B) similarity (C) hate (D) hatred

2. AFFLUENT

    (A) rich (B) destitute (C) poor (D) impoverished

3. ALLOT

    (A) hold (B) refuse (C) distribute (D) withhold

4. ALOOF

    (A) compassionate (B) distant (C) friendly (D) warm

5. AMBIGUOUS

    (A) vague (B) clear (C) certain (D) definite

6. APPARATUS

    (A) reflection (B) device (C) vision (D) appearance

7. ASPIRATION

    (A) apathy (B) hate (C) indifference (D) ambition

8. BOARDER

(A) guest (B) host (C) hostess (D) landlord

9. BROACH

(A) conclude (B) complete (C) begin (D) close

10. CALAMITY

(A) tragedy (B) advantage (C) benefit (D) blessing

11. CLAMMY

(A) moist (B) dry (C) arid (D) barren

12. CONDONE

(A) regard (B) disregard (C) disallow (D) forbid

13. CONSPICUOUS

(A) hidden (B) obscured (C) visible (D) indistinct

14. CONTEMPT

(A) approval (B) esteem (C) flattery (D) dishonor

15. CONTENTION

(A) accord (B) rivalry (C) agreement (D) harmony

16. CONVENE

(A) disperse (B) divide (C) assemble (D) scatter

17. CRASS

(A) vulgar (B) refined (C) polite (D) sophisticated

18. CREDIBLE

(A) deceptive (B) trustworthy (C) dishonest (D) unreliable

19. CUMBERSOME

(A) troublesome (B) convenient (C) fun (D) graceful

20. DELINQUENT

(A) behaved (B) irresponsible (C) careful (D) responsible

21. DETER

(A) allow (B) encourage (C) discourage (D) promote

22. DILIGENT

(A) persistent (B) idle (C) inactive (D) neglectful

23. DISCLOSE

(A) reveal (B) conceal (C) cover (D) deny

24. DISDAIN

(A) admiration (B) dislike (C) approval (D) affection

25. DISMAY

(A) assurance (B) beauty (C) calm (D) apprehension

26. DISSEMINATE

(A) conceal (B) hide (C) disperse (D) collect

27. ENTICE

(A) repel (B) disgust (C) allure (D) dissuade

28. ESOTERIC

(A) private (B) common (C) known (D) public

29. EXPEDITE

(A) accelerate (B) delay (C) hinder (D) slow

30. FACET

(A) tap (B) phase (C) back (D) side

The following questions ask you to find the relationships between words. For each question, select the choice that best completes the meaning of the sentence.

Example

Ann carried the box carefully so that she would not _____ the pretty glasses.

Answer
● Ⓑ Ⓒ Ⓓ

(A) break   (B) fix   (C) open   (D) stop

---

31. Pillow is to blanket as needle is to

    (A) sharp   (B) thread   (C) seamstress   (D) clothes

32. Ear is to earring as bracelet is to

    (A) gold   (B) jewelry   (C) wrist   (D) finger

33. Feet is to socks as head is to

    (A) brain   (B) hair   (C) top   (D) hat

34. Coffee is to cup as food is to

    (A) plate   (B) dinner   (C) biodegradable   (D) kitchen

35. Bread is to toast as egg is to

    (A) chicken   (B) fried   (C) white   (D) fresh

36. Car is to garage as clothes is to

    (A) wear   (B) ironed   (C) launder   (D) closet

37. Books is to bag as pencil is to

    (A) wood   (B) holder   (C) lead   (D) sharpener

38. Laboratory is to microscope as observatory is to

    (A) museum   (B) stars   (C) telescope   (D) science

39. Vine is to grape as tree is to

    (A) green   (B) tall   (C) orange   (D) forest

40. Sky is to stars as sea is to

(A) corals (B) water (C) beach (D) swimming

41. Left is right as front is to

(A) face (B) forward (C) back (D) up

42. Keep is to throw as hide is to

(A) show (B) conceal (C) lock (D) go

43. Effortless is to difficult as obvious is to

(A) doubtful (B) seen (C) glaring (D) evident

44. Fallow is to cultivate as dormant is to

(A) idle (B) active (C) slack (D) neglected

45. Falter is to stabilize as feeble is to

(A) ailing (B) fragile (C) weak (D) healthy

46. Notorious is to unknown as fancy is to

(A) ornate (B) floral (C) plain (D) decorative

47. Formidable is to friendly as frugal is to

(A) careful (B) prudent (C) wasteful (D) economical

48. Futile is to important as gallant is to

(A) coward (B) brave (C) mighty (D) knight

49. Talkative is to silent as polite is to

(A) discourteous (B) amiable (C) cordial (D) courteous

50. Grandiose is to modest as sociable is to

(A) friendly (B) unfriendly (C) party (D) gathering

51. Diamond is to hard as chalk is to

(A) writing (B) brittle (C) board (D) teacher

52. Famine is to hunger as abundance is to

(A) drought (B) farm (C) prosperity (D) money

53. Malevolent is to vicious as benevolent is to

(A) God (B) cruel (C) mean (D) charitable

54. Stubborn is to hard as flexible is to

(A) adaptable (B) adopt (C) firm (D) rigid

55. Hilarious is to funny as dull is to

(A) knife (B) boring (C) brain (D) smart

56. Impeccable is to flawless as faulty is to

(A) well (B) perfect (C) wire (D) defective

57. Imperative is to essential as optional is to

(A) compulsory (B) extra (C) required (D) attendance

58. Impotent is to incompetent as competent is to

(A) competition (B) competitor (C) capable (D) clumsy

59. Inane is to silly as sensible is to

(A) senses (B) funny (C) guess (D) reasonable

60. Incessant is to constant as erratic is to

(A) irregular (B) error (C) machine (D) results

SECTION 5

QUANTITATIVE MATH

Time—30 minutes
25 Questions

In this section, there are five possible answers after each problem. Choose which one is best.

Example

5,413 – 4,827 =

(A) 586
(B) 596
(C) 696
(D) 1,586
(E) 1,686

Answer

● (B) (C) (D) (E)

The correct answer to this question is lettered A, so space A is marked.

1. A right triangle has legs 20 cm and 14 cm. What is the area?

(A) 140 cm   (B) 140 cm²   (C) 280 cm   (D) 410 cm²   (E) 144 cm

2. A basketball team played 20 games, winning 15 of them. What is the ratio of wins to losses?

(A) 3:1   (B) 1:3   (C) 2:1   (D) 1:2   (E) 3:2

3. Evaluate: 24.95 – 35.36 ÷ 4

(A) 16.12   (B) 16.21   (C) 11.16   (D) 16.11   (E) 11.11

4. What is the value of x if $\dfrac{x}{5} = \dfrac{12}{15}$?

(A) 5   (B) 4   (C) 6   (D) 12   (E) 2

5. What is the difference between 81 and the product of 7 and 6?

(A) 15   (B) 10   (C) 13   (D) 17   (E) 20

6. When a number is doubled and the result decreased by five, the number obtained is 17. What is the original number?

(A) 19   (B) 22   (C) 11   (D) 10   (E) 15

7. If $28 < B < 35$ and B is an even whole number, then B could be?

   (A) 33 (B) 29 (C) 36 (D) 31 (E) 34

8. Evaluate: $\sqrt{144} + \sqrt{81} - \sqrt{49}$

   (A) 16 (B) 12 (C) 10 (D) 14 (E) 18

9. Find the range of this set of numbers: 902, 578, 637, 123

   (A) 902 (B) 123 (C) 637 (D) 779 (E) 578

10. The average age of 4 people is 26. What will be the sum of their ages in 3 years?

    (A) 211 (B) 261 (C) 216 (D) 206 (E) cannot be determined

11. What number is halfway between 501 and 509?

    (A) 505 (B) 502 (C) 507 (D) 503 (E) 506

12. Find the median of this set of numbers: 35, 35, 27, 68, 56, 79, 10.

    (A) 10 (B) 35 (C) 68 (D) 56 (E) 79

13. Find the mode of this set of numbers: 127, 345, 901, 901, 345, 574, 403, 901, 403, 715

    (A) 345 (B) 574 (C) 901 (D) 715 (E) 574

14. A standard deck of cards is modified by adding the black jacks from another deck. What is the probability that a card randomly drawn from that modified deck will be a face card (jack, queen, king)?

    (A) $\dfrac{5}{27}$ (B) $\dfrac{14}{27}$ (C) $\dfrac{10}{27}$ (D) $\dfrac{2}{27}$ (E) $\dfrac{7}{27}$

15. Some balls are placed in a box: ten yellow, four red, six blue. What is the probability that a randomly drawn ball will not be blue?

    (A) $\dfrac{2}{27}$ (B) $\dfrac{2}{27}$ (C) $\dfrac{2}{27}$ (D) $\dfrac{2}{27}$ (E) $\dfrac{2}{27}$

16. A pair of fair dice are rolled. What is the probability that the sum will be a multiple of 6?

    (A) $\dfrac{2}{9}$ (B) $\dfrac{7}{9}$ (C) $\dfrac{4}{9}$ (D) $\dfrac{1}{9}$ (E) $\dfrac{8}{9}$

17. Give the slope of the line that passes through $(-2, 4)$ and $(-6, -8)$.

    (A) 8 (B) 6 (C) 3 (D) 5 (E) 10

18. In which quadrant or on which axis of the coordinate plane will you find the point (4, −7)?

(A) quadrant I (B) quadrant II (C) quadrant III (D) quadrant IV (E) none of the above

19. What is the slope of the line that passes through (4, 5) and (2, −1)?

(A) 5 (B) 3 (C) 7 (D) 12 (E) 4.5

20. Zoe wants to build a fence to surround her square garden. The garden has an area of 25 square yards. How much fencing will she need?

(A) 15 yards (B) 18 yards (C) 16 yards (D) 24 yards (E) 20 yards

21. The area of the square is 196 cm. What is the sum of the lengths of three sides of the square?

(A) 42 cm (B) 56 cm (C) 28 cm (D) 34 cm (E) 14 cm

22. What is the area of a square with perimeter 64 in?

(A) 256 in (B) 256 in² (C) 64 in (D) 265 in (E) 46 in²

23. Evaluate: $15.97 + 8.4 \div 2.4$

(A) 10.15 (B) 19.74 (C) 10.51 (D) 19.47 (E) 14.97

24. N is larger than 0. Which of the following could be equal to 2 × N?

I. 42   II. $10\frac{1}{2}$ III. 22.8

(A) I only (B) II only (C) I, II (D) II, III (E) I, II, III

25. Evaluate: $\dfrac{7}{20} + \dfrac{11}{20} - \dfrac{3}{20}$

(A) $\dfrac{3}{10}$ (B) $\dfrac{3}{4}$ (C) $\dfrac{3}{20}$ (D) $\dfrac{7}{20}$ (E) $\dfrac{1}{2}$

Answer Key

Section 1

Topic A: If I were given a superpower, I

In a world where anyone can dream, dreaming of the impossible is both motivational and not. If I were given a superpower, I would pick the power to fly. It must be so freeing to fly just like the birds without a care of what's left behind. Leave all the things behind without a worry and fly as far as your eyes can see. Not worry about these personal belongings that keep us attached to the ground.

If I were to fly, I'd go to places I've never been. I'll go to the places I've only ever dreamed of. Every day is an exciting new view. I will experience to every bit of culture there is in the world. If people were free to fly, we may not be needing fossil fuels to power our vehicles. We may be saving the world from further destruction. There will be no need to wait for ticket sales nor plan in advance. You can fly as soon as you think you needed a much-needed vacation.

I guess the only sad part about being able to fly is the constant want to go somewhere else and not be able to settle. The fear that I might be missing out that there might be more somewhere else. It will be challenging to stay connected with family and to even start your own. Our roots have played an important role to the person we have become and will be. If you were given a chance to pick a superpower, what would your pick?

Section 2

1.	C	6.	D	11.	D	16.	A	21.	C
2.	A	7.	C	12.	B	17.	A	22.	B
3.	B	8.	C	13.	E	18.	A	23.	B
4.	E	9.	E	14.	D	19.	C	24.	C
5.	B	10.	A	15.	B	20.	E	25.	E

1. Answer: C

    Let's distribute 4 to $(x + 15)$ first, then solve for x: $4x + 60 = 120 \Rightarrow 4x = 60 \Rightarrow x = 15$. The value of x is 15, hence the answer is C.

2. Answer: **A**

   Line AE is a straight line so, if we add line segments AB, BC, CD and DE, the sum would be equal to AE.

   $x + x + 2 + 3x + 6 + x - 10 = 64 \implies 6x - 2 = 64 \implies 6x = 66 \implies x = 11$. Line segment AB $= x$ and $x = 11$, hence AB = 11 cm. The answer is A.

3. Answer: **B**

   Let's first get the area of bigger square and the area of the smaller square. To get the area of the squares, use the formula $A = s^2$. For the bigger square: $A = 9^2 = 81$. For the smaller square: $A = 3^2 = 9$. Let's then divide the area of the bigger square by the smaller square to get the number of smaller squares that can be cut out from the bigger square. $81 \div 9 = 9$. We can create 9 smaller squares, hence the answer is B.

4. Answer: **E**

   The formula to get the perimeter of a square is $P = 4s$. Substitute the value of P (perimeter) to get the length of the sides: $170.8 = 4s \implies s = 42.7$. The length of one side of the square is 42.7 cm, hence the answer is E.

5. Answer: **B**

   Let's first convert these mixed fractions to improper fractions, then get the reciprocal of the divisor and change the sign to multiplication.: $3\frac{4}{7} \div 2\frac{6}{7} = \frac{25}{7} \div \frac{20}{7} = \frac{25}{7} \div \frac{7}{20} = \frac{175}{140} = \frac{5}{4}$ or $1\frac{1}{4}$. The quotient is $1\frac{1}{4}$, hence the answer is B.

6. Answer: **D**

   To get the decimal form of a fraction, divide the numerator with the denominator: $19 \div 500 = 0.038$. The answer is D.

7. Answer: **C**

   After two years, each person will be two years older. Since there are three of them, their ages will be 3×2 years more. We can add 6 to the original total of 33 to get their total age after two years: $33 + 6 = 39$. The sum of their ages after two years will be 39, hence the answer is C.

8. Answer: **C**

   Using PEMDAS rule, we need to solve the equation inside the parenthesis first, then subtract: $37 - (6 \times 4) = 37 - 24 = 13$. The answer is C.

9. Answer: **E**

   Find the value of x: $x - 37 = 73 \implies x = 110$. The value of x is 110, hence the answer is E.

10. Answer: **A**

    Sarah initially borrowed 54 books. When she returned half of it, she was left with 27 books. She then borrowed another 7 books. With the remaining books she has and the additional 7 books she borrowed, she has now a total of 34 books, hence the answer is A.

11. Answer: D

   Using the PEMDAS rule, we need to multiply the expression first, then add and subtract, hence the answer is D.

12. Answer: B

   To get the amount that Leonard paid for the pencil, simply subtract the change he received from the dollar bill he used to pay. We can put it an expression of $10 - b$, hence the answer is B.

13. Answer: E

   To get the value of z, use cross-multiplication: $75z = 450 \Rightarrow z = 6$. The value of z is 6, hence the answer is E.

14. Answer: D

   To get the area of a parallelogram, use the formula $A = b \times h = 20 \times 9 = 180$. The area of the parallelogram is 180 cm², hence the answer is D.

15. Answer: B

   To get the perimeter of the parallelogram, use the formula $P = 2a + 2b = 2(19) + 2(23) = 38 + 46 = 84$. The perimeter of the parallelogram is 84 in, hence the answer is B.

16. Answer: A

   To get the volume of a cube, use the formula $V = s^3 = 8^3 = 512$. The volume of the cube is 512 cm³, hence the answer is A.

17. Answer: A

   If $\frac{1}{8}$ of a pound of sugar costs $3.00, then the price for a pound will be 8 times as much. Multiply $3.00 with 8: $3 \times 8 = 24$. The price for a pound of sugar is $24.00, hence the answer is A.

18. Answer: A

   Let x be the number. $\frac{120}{100}x = 126 \Rightarrow 1.2x = 126 \Rightarrow x = 105$. The number is 105, hence the answer is A.

19. Answer: C

   To get the area of a rectangle, use the formula $A = lw$. Substitute the value of Area (A) and width (w) to get the length (l): $120 = l \times 10 \Rightarrow l = 12$. Now that we have the length, we can solve for the perimeter. $P = 2l + 2w = 2(12) + 2(10) = 24 + 20 = 44$. The perimeter of rectangle KLMN is 44 cm, hence the answer is C.

20. Answer: **E**

To get the perimeter of a rectangle, we use the formula $P = 2l + 2w$. It was given that the width is half of the length, so the length (in terms of w) will be $2w$. If we substitute it to the l in the equation, we will then have $P = 2(2w) + 2w = 4w + 2w = 6w$. The perimeter of the rectangle in terms of w is $6w$, hence the answer is E.

21. Answer: **C**

To convert percent to fraction, divide the percentage by 100. We will have $\frac{75}{100}$ and the simplest form of $\frac{3}{4}$, hence the answer is C.

22. Answer: **B**

To divide fractions, get the reciprocal of the divisor and change the operation to multiplication: $\frac{3}{5} \div \frac{9}{10} = \frac{3}{5} \times \frac{10}{9} = \frac{30}{45} = \frac{2}{3}$. The quotient is $\frac{2}{3}$, hence the answer is B.

23. Answer: **B**

Distribute -3 to $(-2x + 9)$: $-3(-2x) + -3(9) = 6x - 27$. The answer is B.

24. Answer: **C**

Distributive property indicates that for any values of $a, b, c, a(b + c) = a \times b + a \times c$. Among the choices, only option C exhibits this rule, hence the answer is C.

25. Answer: **E**

Find the difference: $212 - 157.67 = 54.33$. The difference is 54.33, hence the answer is E.

Section 3

1.	A	7.	C	13.	A	19.	C	25.	B	31.	B	37.	B
2.	B	8.	A	14.	B	20.	A	26.	C	32.	C	38.	C
3.	C	9.	A	15.	C	21.	A	27.	D	33.	D	39.	D
4.	D	10.	B	16.	D	22.	B	28.	A	34.	A	40.	A
5.	D	11.	D	17.	D	23.	D	29.	B	35.	B		
6.	B	12.	C	18.	B	24.	C	30.	D	36.	D		

1.   The correct answer is A. "Sabbath" is the Lord's day, therefore a rest day. This is why John did not accept the work offered at the large shop.

2.   The correct answer is B. He returned the favor by offering John a job; therefore, we may assume that he is grateful for John's deed.

3. The correct answer is C. John is displayed as a kind-hearted boy in the passage who is honest and cares for his mother.

4. The correct answer is D. John went home with his heart and his eyes so full after receiving the good news of the job opportunity; therefore, the feeling was happiness.

5. The correct answer is D. "Were" is the past tense of the verb "are." It is the plural form of "is" (simple) and "was" (past).

6. The correct answer is B. John didn't accept the place at the large shop because they kept the shop open on Sabbath, and mother would not wish John to work on the Lord's day.

7. The correct answer is C. "Distress" is great pain, anxiety, or sorrow; acute physical or mental suffering; affliction; trouble. It is a state of extreme necessity or misfortune.

8. The correct answer is A. The phrase "that many a brave, loving heart has ceased to beat forever" came after the phrase that hundreds are thought to have perished, which means many people are thought to be dead.

9. The correct answer is A. The word "dawns" was used in the phrase "Morning dawns," which meant morning came. To dawn means to begin to grow light in the morning.

10. The correct answer is B. "To glean" means to gather slowly and laboriously, bit by bit.

11. The correct answer is D. "Audible" means capable of being heard; loud enough to be heard; actually heard.

12. The correct answer is C. The passage described a day after distress when people came to the beach early in the morning to check if for wreck washed ashore.

13. The correct answer is A. "Feeble" means lacking in volume, loudness, brightness, or distinctness.

14. The correct answer is B. The children were playing by the stream when they saw a kitten in the rushing water.

15. The correct answer is C. "To drench" means to wet thoroughly; soak.

16. The correct answer is D. Quick as a flash Dick ran off the bridge, which means the little boy ran very quickly to save the kitten.

17. The correct answer is D. "Clung" is the past tense of the verb "cling." To cling means to hold on tightly to.

18. The correct answer is B. "Wretched" means (of a person) in a very unhappy or unfortunate state.

19. The correct answer is C. President Joe Biden has made electric vehicles (EVs) a priority to promote zero-emission vehicles as a response to the climate crisis. A few readers were asked their opinion, and there were mixed opinions.

20. The correct answer is A. President Joe Biden has made electric vehicles (EVs) a priority.

21. The correct answer is A. The United States is one the biggest emitters of greenhouse gases, which more than a quarter of the country's emissions come from gasoline-burning vehicles.

22. The correct answer is B. For now, most people plan to stick with gas-powered vehicles because EVs are expensive and charging them is a hassle.

23. The correct answer is D. The article presented both opinions of the readers who were asked about their thoughts on EVs.

24. The correct answer is C. Sputnik, the world's first satellite.

25. The correct answer is B. Sputnik was launched in October 1957.

26. The correct answer is C. The researchers are calling for a global treaty to limit the amount of junk in space that poses a threat to spacecraft.

27. The correct answer is D. The global treaty wishes to limit the amount of junk in space that poses a threat to spacecraft.

28. The correct answer is A. 100 trillion human-made objects are circling the planet now.

29. The correct answer is B. A treaty is a formal agreement between two or more states in reference to peace, alliance, commerce, or other international relations.

30. The correct answer is D. 16 young people are suing the state of Montana for the state policy to increase fossil fuel development.

31. The correct answer is B. The article provides information on the first youth climate case in the United States.

32. The correct answer is C. Sixteen young people are suing the state of Montana for the state policy to increase fossil fuel development, which is a clear violation of the right to a clean and health environment.

33. The correct answer is D. The kids ranged in age from 2 to 18.

34. The correct answer is A. "To repeal" is to revoke or annul (a law, tax, duty, etc.) by express legislative enactment; abrogate.

35. The correct answer is B. *Held v. Montana* is not the first youth climate case in the United States. But it's the first to go to trial.

36. The correct answer is D. The article talked about an Arizona desert community experiencing drought and the many ideas on how to procure water for the community, along with the possible environmental threats they pose.

37. The correct answer is B. It gets water from the Colorado River. But the river is drying up.

38. The correct answer is C. Supporters say the solutions could provide water for decades. Critics see a different future: environmental destruction.

39. The correct answer is D. "Drought" means a period of dry weather, especially a long one that is injurious to crops; an extended shortage.

40. The correct answer is A. Arizona can pump water from underground. But that can't provide half of what's needed.

Section 4

1. B	11. A	21. C	31. B	41. C	51. B
2. A	12. B	22. A	32. C	42. A	52. C
3. C	13. C	23. A	33. D	43. A	53. D
4. B	14. D	24. B	34. A	44. B	54. A
5. A	15. B	25. D	35. B	45. D	55. B
6. B	16. C	26. C	36. D	46. C	56. D
7. D	17. A	27. C	37. B	47. C	57. B
8. A	18. B	28. A	38. C	48. A	58. C
9. C	19. A	29. A	39. D	49. A	59. D
10. A	20. B	30. B	40. A	50. B	60. A

1. The correct answer is B. "Affinity" means a natural liking for or attraction to a person, thing, idea, etc. Synonyms are affection and similarity.

2. The correct answer is A. "Affluent" means having an abundance of wealth, property, or other material goods; prosperous; rich.

3. The correct answer is C. "To allot" means to divide or distribute by share or portion; distribute or parcel out.

4. The correct answer is B. "Aloof" means at a distance, especially in feeling or interest. Synonyms are distant and detached.

5. The correct answer is A. "Ambiguous" means open to or having several possible meanings or interpretations. Synonyms are unclear and vague.

6. The correct answer is B. An apparatus is any complex instrument or mechanism for a particular purpose.

7. The correct answer is D. "Aspiration" is a strong desire, longing, or aim; ambition.

8. The correct answer is A. "A boarder" is a person, especially a lodger. Synonyms are paying guest and renter.

9. The correct answer is C. "To broach" means to mention or suggest for the first time. Synonyms are to begin and crack.

10. The correct answer is A. "A calamity" is a great misfortune or disaster, as a flood or serious injury; a tragedy.

11. The correct answer is A. "Clammy" means covered with a cold, sticky moisture; cold and damp; moist.

12. The correct answer is B. "To condone" means to disregard or overlook (something illegal, objectionable, or the like).

13. The correct answer is C. "Conspicuous" means easily seen or noticed; readily visible or observable.

14. The correct answer is D. "Contempt" is the state of being despised; dishonor; disgrace.

15. The correct answer is B. "Contention" is a striving in rivalry; competition; contest.

16. The correct answer is C. "To convene" means to come together or assemble, usually for some public purpose.

17. The correct answer is A. "Crass" means without refinement, delicacy, or sensitivity; gross; obtuse; stupid.

18. The correct answer is B. "Credible" means worthy of belief or confidence; trustworthy.

19. The correct answer is A. "Cumbersome" means burdensome; troublesome.

20. The correct answer is B. "Delinquent" means failing in or neglectful of a duty or obligation; guilty of a misdeed or offense. Synonyms are irresponsible and careless.

21. The correct answer is C. "To deter" means to discourage or restrain from acting or proceeding. Synonyms are to block and dissuade.

22. The correct answer is A. "Diligent" means constant in effort to accomplish something; attentive and persistent in doing anything. Synonyms are eager and persistent.

23. The correct answer is A. "To disclose" means to make known; reveal or uncover.

24. The correct answer is B. "Disdain" is a feeling of contempt for anything regarded as unworthy; haughty contempt; scorn. Synonyms are dislike and hatred.

25. The correct answer is D. "Dismay" is sudden or complete loss of courage; utter disheartenment. Synonyms are apprehension and panic.

26. The correct answer is C. "To disseminate" means to scatter or spread widely, as though sowing seed; promulgate extensively; broadcast; disperse.

27. The correct answer is C. "To entice" means to lead on by exciting hope or desire; allure; inveigle.

28. The correct answer is A. "Esoteric" means private; secret; confidential.

29. The correct answer is A. "To expedite" means to speed up the progress of; hasten. Synonyms are to accelerate and quicken.

30. The correct answer is B. A facet is an aspect; phase.

31. The correct answer is B. The first word pair is items that you use together for the same purpose/action. Pillow and blanket for sleeping; needle and thread for sewing.

32. The correct answer is C. The first word pair has body part–jewelry relationship. An earring is for your ear; a bracelet is for your wrist.

33. The correct answer is D. The first word pair has body part–garment relationship. Socks are for your feet; a hat is for your head.

34. The correct answer is A. The first word pair has food–kitchenware relationship. You drink coffee in a cup; eat food in a plate.

35. The correct answer is B. The first word pair has food–cooking method relationship. Bread can be toast; eggs are fried.

36. The correct answer is D. The first word pair has item–place relationship. Cars are parked in a garage when not in use; clothes are kept in a closet.

37. The correct answer is B. The first word pair has item–place relationship. Books are carried in a bag; pencils are kept in a case.

38. The correct answer is C. The first word pair has place–equipment relationship. Microscopes are used in laboratories; telescopes are used in observatories.

39. The correct answer is D. The first word pair has type–plant relationship. Grape is a vine; orange is a tree.

40. The correct answer is A. The first word pair has place–object relationship. Stars are observed in the sky; corals grow at the bottom of the sea.

41. The correct answer is C. The first word pair is antonyms. Front is the opposite of back.

42. The correct answer is A. The first word pair is antonyms. Hide is the opposite of show.

43. The correct answer is A. The first word pair is antonyms. Obvious is the opposite of doubtful.

44. The correct answer is B. The first word pair is antonyms. Fallow means plowed and left unseeded for a season or more; uncultivated. Dormant means inactive.

45. The correct answer is D. The first word pair is antonyms. To falter means to hesitate. Feeble means not strong; ineffective

46. The correct answer is C. The first word pair is antonyms. Notorious means unfavorably famous. Fancy means ornamental; decorative; not plain.

47. The correct answer is C. The first word pair is antonyms. Formidable means of discouraging or awesome strength, size, difficulty, etc.; intimidating. Frugal means economical in use or expenditure; prudently saving or sparing; not wasteful.

48. The correct answer is A. The first word pair is antonyms. Futile means incapable of producing any result; ineffective; useless; not successful. Gallant means brave, spirited, noble-minded, or chivalrous.

49. The correct answer is A. The first word pair is antonyms. Polite means mannerly, civilized.

50. The correct answer is B. The first word pair is antonyms. Grandiose means affectedly grand or important; pompous.

51. The correct answer is B. The first word pair has object–characteristic relationship. A diamond is hard; a chalk is brittle.

52. The correct answer is C. The first word pair is synonyms. Famine means any extreme and general scarcity. Abundance means overflowing fullness.

53. The correct answer is D. The first word pair is synonyms. Malevolent means wishing evil or harm to another or others. Benevolent means desiring to help others.

54. The correct answer is A. The first word pair is synonyms. Stubborn means hard, tough, or stiff, as stone or wood; difficult to shape or work. Flexible means susceptible of modification or adaptation.

55. The correct answer is B. The first word pair is synonyms. Hilarious means boisterously merry or cheerful. Dull means uninteresting.

56. The correct answer is D. The first word pair is synonyms. Impeccable means faultless; flawless; irreproachable. Faulty means broken, not working

57. The correct answer is B. The first word pair is synonyms. Imperative means absolutely necessary or required; unavoidable. Optional means possible; available as choice.

58. The correct answer is C. The first word pair is synonyms. Impotent means not potent; lacking power or ability. Competent means having suitable or sufficient skill, knowledge, experience, etc., for some purpose; properly qualified.

59. The correct answer is D. The first word pair is synonyms. Inane means lacking sense, significance, or ideas. Sensible means having, using, or showing good sense or sound judgment.

60. The correct answer is A. The first word pair is synonyms. Incessant means inconsistent, irregular, or unpredictable. Erratic means inconsistent, irregular, or unpredictable

Section 5

1.	B	6.	C	11.	A	16.	D	21.	A
2.	A	7.	E	12.	B	17.	C	22.	B
3.	D	8.	D	13.	C	18.	D	23.	D
4.	B	9.	D	14.	E	19.	B	24.	E
5.	C	10.	C	15.	A	20.	E	25.	B

1. Answer: **B**

   The legs of a right triangle are its base and height. To get the area of a triangle, use the formula $A = \frac{1}{2}bh = \frac{1}{2}(14)(20) = 140 \text{ cm}^2$. The area of the right triangle is 140 cm², hence the answer is B.

2. Answer: **A**

   To get the ratio of wins to losses, we need to know first how many games they lost. Since they win 15 games out of 20, then we can get number of losses by subtracting 15 from 20: 20 – 15 = 5. They lost 5 times. We can now get the ratio; 15:5 = 3:1. The ratio is 3:1, hence the answer is A.

3. Answer: **D**

   Using the PEMDAS rule, we need to divide first, then subtract: 24.95 – 35.36 ÷ 4 = 24.95 – 8.84 = 16.11. The answer is D.

4. Answer: **B**

   To get the value of x, use cross-multiplication: $15x = 60 \Rightarrow x = 4$. The value of x is 4, hence the answer is B.

5. Answer: **C**

   Using PEMDAS rule, we need to solve the equation inside the parenthesis first, then subtract: 81 – (7 × 6) = 81 – 42 = 39. The answer is C.

6. Answer: **C**

   Let x be the number. $2x – 5 = 17 \Rightarrow 2x = 22 \Rightarrow x = 11$. The number is 11, hence the answer is C.

7. Answer: **E**

   It was given that B is greater than 28 but less than 35, so B is a number between 28 and 35. It was also given that B is an even number. Among the choices, only option E exhibits these criteria, hence the answer is E.

8. Answer: **D**

Let's get the square root first, then solve: $\sqrt{144} + \sqrt{81} - \sqrt{49} = 12 + 9 - 7 = 14$. The answer is D.

9. Answer: **D**

Range, in mathematics and statistics, is the difference between the maximum and minimum values of a data set. The highest value in the given set is 902 and the lowest value is 123. Let's subtract the two values: 902 – 123 = 779. The range is 779, hence the answer is D.

10. Answer: **C**

Since the average age of these people is 26, then the sum of their current ages is 4 × 26 = 204. These four people will gain three years in age, then we need to add 12 to the sum of their current ages: 204 + 12 = 216. The sum of their ages after 3 years is 216, hence the answer is C.

11. Answer: **A**

To get the halfway between 501 and 509, we can add the two numbers and then divide the sum by two to get the middle number: $\dfrac{501 + 509}{2} = \dfrac{1010}{2} = 505$. The answer is A.

12. Answer: **B**

The median is the middlemost value in the ordered list. Let's rearrange the given list in ascending order {10, 27, 35, 35, 56, 68, 79}. Since there are seven numbers, the 4th number is the middlemost value so the median is 35. The answer is B.

13. Answer: **C**

Mode is the most frequently occurring value. Let's rearrange the given list in ascending order {127, 345, 345, 403, 403, 574, 715, 901, 901, 901}. The most frequent data on the set is 901, hence the mode is 901. The answer is C.

14. Answer: **E**

There are 12 face cards (4 jacks, 4 queens, and 4 kings) in a 52-card standard deck. If we will add two black jacks, then we will now have 14 face cards and we will have a total of 54 cards on hand. The probability of getting a face card will be $\dfrac{14}{54}$ or $\dfrac{7}{27}$, hence the answer is E.

15. Answer: **A**

Let's get the total balls in the box: 10 yellow + 4 red + 6 blue = 20 balls. Since we need to randomly pick either a yellow ball or red ball, we need to add the number of yellow and red balls: 10 + 4 = 14. The probability of not getting a blue ball will be $\dfrac{14}{20}$ or $\dfrac{14}{20}$, hence the answer is A.

16. **Answer: D**

    There are three possible multiples of 6 that can come out: 6 and 12. These are the possible outcomes which will result in a multiple of 6:

    6: (1,5), (2,4), (3,3)

    12: (6,6)

    There are 36 equally probable outcomes for a pair of dice, so the probability of getting a sum with a multiple of 6 will be $\frac{4}{36}$ or $\frac{1}{9}$, hence the answer is D.

17. **Answer: C**

    To get the slope, we can use the formula $m = \frac{y_2 - y_1}{x_2 - x_1} = \frac{-8 - 4}{-6 - (-2)} = \frac{-12}{-4} = 3$. The slope is 3, hence the answer is C.

18. **Answer: D**

    A point with a positive x-coordinate and a negative y-coordinate can be found in Quadrant IV, hence the answer is D.

19. **Answer: B**

    To get the slope, we can use the formula $m = \frac{y_2 - y_1}{x_2 - x_1} = \frac{-8 - 5}{2 - 4} = \frac{-6}{-2} = 3$. The slope is 3, hence the answer is B.

20. **Answer: E**

    To get the length of the fence Zoe needs, we need to get the perimeter of the garden. The area was given, so we just need to get the length of each side. $A = s^2 \Rightarrow s = \sqrt{25} = 5$ yards. Now that we have the length of one side, we can solve for the perimeter: $P = 4s = 4(5) = 20$ yards. Zoe needs 20 yards to fence her garden, hence the answer is E.

21. **Answer: A**

    We need to get the length of each side. $A = s^2 \Rightarrow s = \sqrt{196} = 14$ cm. Each side measures 14 cm. Multiply it by three to get the sum of the three sides: $14 \times 3 = 42$ cm. The answer is A.

22. **Answer: B**

    We need to get the length of each side. $P = 4s \Rightarrow 64 = 4s \Rightarrow s = 16$ in. Now that we have the length of each side, solve for the area: $A = s^2 = 16^2 = 256$ in^2. The area of the square is 256 in^2, hence the answer is B.

23. **Answer: D**

    Using PEMDAS rule, we need to divide first before we add: $15.97 + 8.4 \div 2.4 = 15.97 + 3.5 = 19.47$. The answer is D.

24. Answer: **E**

The only condition given is that N is greater than 0, so N could be any positive integer. All choices could be the product, hence the answer is E.

25. Answer: **B**

To evaluate fractions with same denominator, copy the value of the denominator and solve for the operation in the numerator. Get the simplest form: $\dfrac{7}{20} + \dfrac{11}{20} - \dfrac{3}{20} = \dfrac{7+11-3}{20} = \dfrac{15}{20} = \dfrac{3}{4}$. Answer is B.

SSAT Report

Scoring Methodology

On the **Middle and Upper Level SSAT**, a point is awarded for each correct answer, a quarter of a point is subtracted for each incorrect answer, and no points are awarded or deducted for omitted questions.

On the **Elementary Level SSAT**, a point is awarded for each correct answer and there is no penalty for incorrect answers.

Score Report Breakdown

Personal Information

The score report header details the student's basic information—name, address, date of birth, gender, etc. Enrollment Management Association (EMA) will have scored the student at the grade displayed as indicated during registration. Please note that while gender is listed, SSAT scores are not gender-specific.

Total Score Summary

This section lists the two total scores.

"**Your score**" is the total scaled score, and the pointer indicates where the student's score is between the highest and lowest possible score. We also provide the average score for additional context.

The **total percentile** is on the right, comparing the student's scaled score to other SSAT test takers. This score shows the percentage of students that the student scored equal to or higher. For example, a 67th percentile indicates that the student scored equal to or higher than sixty-seven percent of test-takers in their grade.

Section Scores

In this section, EMA breaks score information into verbal, quantitative (math), and reading segments. Similar to the total score, a scaled score and percentile are shown, along with the average score. We also provide a score range; students who retest within a short period will likely score within this range. A breakdown explaining the main types of questions follows, including the number of questions answered correctly, incorrectly, and unanswered.

Here's a sample SSAT Report